AF564699

REGIONAL STOCK EXCHANGES IN INDIA

Strategies for Revival

REGIONAL STOCK EXCHANGES IN INDIA

STRATEGIES FOR REVIVAL

NARDEEP KUMAR MAHESHWARY
Professor-cum-Director,
SAS Institute of Information Technology,
SAS Nagar, Mohali,
Chandigarh

DEEP & DEEP PUBLICATIONS PVT. LTD.
F-159, Rajouri Garden, New Delhi-110027

REGIONAL STOCK EXCHANGES IN INDIA

ISBN 978-81-8450-379-1

Typeset by S.S. COMPOSERS
3190, Mohindra Park, Shakur Basti, Delhi-110034.

Printed in India at MAYUR ENTERPRISES
WZ Plot No. 3, Gujjar Market, Tihar Village, New Delhi-110018.

Published by DEEP & DEEP PUBLICATIONS PVT. LTD.
F-159, Rajouri Garden, New Delhi-110027.
Phones: 25435369, 25440916
E-mail: ddpbooks@yahoo.co.in • ddpubs@gmail.com
Showroom:
2/13, Ansari Road, Daryaganj, New Delhi-110002 • Telefax: 23245122

Contents

PREFACE

Indian securities market has large number of stocks. With the recent reforms in the securities markets, regional stock exchanges have lost their business, making it harder for them to provide the liquidity. How to overcome this problem has been engaging the attention of regulators and the national level stock exchanges. Several rounds of discussions have also taken place among the representatives of regional stock exchanges on the best form of business model they should design in order to make them more relevant in the background of intense competition and heavy focus on technology.

As in several other fields, technology drives today the stock markets the world over. India is no exception. Establishment of National Stock Exchange (NSE) in 1994 with an all India spread throughout the country and expansion of operations of Bombay Stock Exchange (BSE), both of which have their trader work stations at over 400 centers in the country today, have led to virtual extinction of all the 19 regional stock exchanges spread across the length and breadth of the country. At present, there is virtually no trading at any of these regional stock exchanges.

With a view to revive small regional stock exchanges, Securities and Exchange Board of India the regulatory body came out with alternatives for survival of these regional exchanges but efforts made by the regulator for revival of regional stock exchanges have not bore results.

The present book is an attempt to look into revival of regional stock exchanges and suggest the revival strategies for the same.

The book is organized in four chapters.

Chapter 1 is the introduction to the study and deals with the evolution of the stock exchange as an institution. The discussion is divided into two parts. Section I is devoted to the introduction of stock exchanges in India and traces the growth and development of regional stock exchanges in the country. It also highlights the role, problems and prospects of the regional stock exchanges in the country. Section II focuses on the history and growth pattern of stock exchanges in the world. The emphasis is primarily on the emergence of stock exchanges across the globe.

Chapter 2 is an attempt to analyze and interpret the performance evaluation of regional stock exchanges from the secondary and primary data. The tools used for data collection have been analyzed using techniques like simple averages, weighted average and factor analysis. The results are suitably interpreted.

Chapter 3 discusses the revival strategies of the stock exchanges. It discusses the diversification and re-organization strategies of regional stock exchanges.

Chapter 4 deals with the conclusions and suggestions. This chapter also discusses the alternative theoretical models of the future stock exchanges.

NARDEEP KUMAR MAHESHWARY

ACKNOWLEDGEMENTS

Pursuing a research project is both a painful and enjoyable experience. It's just like climbing a high peak, step by step, accompanied with frustrations, hardships, encouragement and trust and so many people's kind help and lastly heavenly blessings. When I found myself at the top enjoying the beautiful scenery, I realized that it was, in fact, teamwork that got me there. Though it will not be enough to express my gratitude in words to all those people who helped me, I would still like to give many, many thanks to all of them.

I would like to extend my sincere gratitude and indebtness to my honourable supervisor Dr. H.L.Verma, Professor, Haryana School of Business, who accepted me as his Ph.D. student without hesitation when I presented him my research proposal. Thereafter he offered me all valuable advice and guidance during the course of completion and I owe my learning to him and admit that I could not have finished my dissertation successfully without his support and constant encouragement.

I offer my heart felt thanks and gratitude to my co-supervisor and mentor Dr. B.S. Bhatia, Sr. Professor and Director General, Regional Institute of Management and Computer Technology (RIMT), Mandi Gobindgarh. I owe this research work to him, who has been a constant source of inspiration to a young researcher like me and has always extended his full co-operation and support during this academic pursuit. It was his constant encouragement that made me feel confident that I would be able to overcome every hurdle during accomplishment of my task.

I am highly grateful to Sh. H.S. Sidhu, MD, Delhi Stock

Exchange, Ms. Pooja Sharma, CEO, Ludhiana Stock Exchange, Ms. Usha Sharma, GM, Jaipur Stock Exchange and Ms. Seema Gusain for having extended all support and co-operation for completion of my research and helping me in data collection. I would also place on record my deep sense of appreciation for all the other officials and staffs of these stock exchanges. I also thank all the brokers, professionals, investors, researchers and academicians who have been a part of this research.

I would also like to express my thanks to all the faculty members and staff of Haryana School of Business, Guru Jambheshwar University of Science and Technology, Hisar for having provided me with this opportunity and extending me all support and guidance for completion of my thesis.

I would like to convey my special thanks to Dr. S.C. Kundu, Director, Haryana School of Business, Dr. M.C. Garg, Reader, Haryana School of Business and Prof. Surender Singh, Director, RIMT, School of Management Studies for their academic input and valuable guidance during the course of thesis completion.

I am failing on words to express my feelings for heavenly blessings showered on me by my late parents Sh. J.K. Maheshwary and Smt. Neeta Devi, to whom I owe my life. Their heavenly support and encouragement have always stood by me, as usual, during all my endeavors.

I express my deep sense of emotions for my loving and caring family members including my wife Manisha and my children Akshit and Kashika, for bearing my neglect and instead providing me wholehearted support for completion of my research work.

Lastly, I stand before the almighty with folded hands and fail to express my gratitude towards him for providing the energy and strength to complete the task.

NARDEEP KUMAR MAHESHWARY

LIST OF ABBREVIATIONS

ADR	American Depository Receipt
ASEAN	Association of South East Asian Nations
BOLT	Bombay Online Trading
BRIC	Brazil Russia India China
BSE	Bombay Stock Exchange
CCI	Controller of Capital Issues
CD	Certificate of Deposits
CDSL	Central Depository Services Limited
CRISIL	Credit Rating Information Services of India Limited
OCTEI	Over The Counter Exchange of India
DCA	Department of Company Affairs
DEA	Department of Economic Affairs
DEX	The Diversified Exchange
DIP	Disclosure and Investors Protection Guidelines
DJIA	Dow Jones Industrial Average
ECBs	External Commercial Borrowings
ECFM	Exchange Certificate in Financial Markets
EPS	Earning Per Share
ESOP	Employee Stock Option Plans
FCCBs	Fully Convertible Currency Bonds
FDI	Foreign Direct Investment
FIBV	Federation Internationale Des Bourses De Valeurs
FIIs	Foreign Institutional Investors
FISE	Federation of Indian Stock Exchange
GDP	Gross Domestic Product
GDR	Global Depository Receipt
GEX	The Global Exchange
ICSE	Inter Connected Stock Exchanges
IEPF	Investor Education and Protection Fund

IPO	Initial Public Offer
ISE	Inter Connected Stock Exchanges
LSE	London Stock Exchange
MCX	Multi Commodity Exchange
NAFTA	North American Free Trade Agreement
NASDAQ	National Association of Securities Dealers Automated Quotations
NCDEX	National Commodity and Derivatives Exchange Limited
NSCCL	National Security Clearing Corporation Limited
NSDL	National Securities Depository Limited
NSE	National Stock Exchange
NSEIL	National Stock Exchange of India Limited
NYSE	New York Stock Exchange
OCBs	Overseas Corporate Bodies
PE Ratio	Price Earning Ratio
RBI	Reserve Bank of India
REX	The Regional Exchange
RITs	Retail Individual Investors
RSE	Regional Stock Exchanges
SAARC	South Asian Association for Regional Cooperation
SBTS	Screen-based Trading System
SBU	Strategic Business Unit
SCRA	Securities Contract Regulation Act
SEBI	Securities and Exchange Board of India
SEC	Security and Exchange Commision
SGF	Settlement Guarantee Fund
SME	Small and Medium Enterprises
SPSS	Statistical Package for Social Sciences
TSE	Toronto Stock Exchange
TYSE	Tokyo Stock Exchange
UNCTAD	United Nations Conference on Trade and Development

INTRODUCTION

This chapter deals with the evolution of the stock exchange as an institution. The discussion is divided into two parts. Section I is devoted to the introduction of stock exchanges and trace the growth and development of regional stock exchanges in the country. It also highlights the role, problems and prospects of the regional stock exchanges in India. Section II focuses on the history and growth pattern of stock exchanges in the world. The emphasis is primarily on the emergence of stock exchanges across the globe.

1.1 INTRODUCTION OF STOCK EXCHANGES

1.1.1 Evolution of Stock Exchanges

Stock exchange is an institution evolved in industrially developed capitalist economies with free market mechanism.[1] The idea of commercial enterprise in which risk and profit are shared between financiers and traders as joint participants is very old. Wealthy nobles and merchants in Greece and Rome and later in the Italian city states used to contribute to the initial outlay and trading expeditions and ventures undertaken by ship-owners and other traders in return for a share of the eventual profit.

The legal rules for the 'Commanda', perhaps the

earliest formalised system of commercial joint enterprise, facilitated this type of transaction by allowing the liability of the investor, who had no control over the conduct of the venture, to be limited to the amount he had contributed. Roman lawyers also developed the concept of an association, the 'societas', with legal rights and duties independent of its individual members, which laid the foundation of the modern idea of the corporate form as a separate legal entity.

The structure of the modern company has therefore, been derived more or less directly from the concepts of the 'Commanda' and the 'Societas'.[2] International trade led entrepreneurs to pool their resources. Such joint ventures took place, in which several members of the company would pool their resources in a single expedition and in time.

It came to be an accepted practice for the company itself to organise the various ventures for which members would be entitled or expected to contribute money or goods. This type of venture came to be known as joint stock, since each member instead of trading with his own stock agreed to pool it in a common enterprise. In this process grew the enterprises in which each member was free to trade as he pleased, subject to the rules of the enterprise. The joint stock system became popular in other spheres for the operation of any new trading venture which required a large initial capital. When capital was raised on a wide scale, there emerged demands and pressures from investors to have means, by which they can get their initial contribution, when they wished. A public market, in which an investor can recover his contribution, came into existence. The much wider base for the raising of capital which the capital market permitted was soon reflected in the proliferation of joint stock enterprises in the 1690s and early 1700s.

A major breakthrough in the history of joint stock company form of organisation came in 1856, when the concept of limited liability was introduced in U.K. From 1856 any company which complied with the terms of the Companies Act and added the word 'Limited' to its formal title, such a company was entitled to limit its liability and that of its members, to the amount of its subscribed capital. Joint stock companies came to dominate the economic scene from the mid-nineteenth century. Fast expanding industrialisation during that period needed huge capital. It was being increasingly felt that the finance needed for business activity could not be supplied only by entrepreneurs' themselves.[3]

Then the process of replacement of the solitary entrepreneur by larger and larger joint stock companies became faster. In typical free market, the individual investor would ideally choose to make money available to those new or existing enterprises which offer the best prospect of immediate and continuing profit.

Since he is entitled to withdraw his money from a less profitable enterprise by selling his shares, as long as he can find a buyer and to reinvest it, he will be continually looking for new and more profitable outlets for his money. Therefore, in theory, stock exchange was termed as institutional allocator of resources par excellence.[4]

The proper achievement of this function however is dependent on a number of factors like freedom for individual investors to allocate their capital within the market as they please. It must also be so organised that those who deal with it are fully informed of all the relevant details of the enterprise in which they are being asked to invest. Further, the investor should be free to withdraw his money from a particular company and reinvest it in another or use his money in other ways as and when he wishes to do so.

Briefly, in western capitalist economies, the stock exchange became an institution broadly fulfiling the following objectives:

(i) Making funds available to entrepreneurs for business activity;
(ii) Ensuring maximum return on the investment made by the investors;
(iii) Providing platform for saving, investment and reinvestment activity; and
(iv) Ensuring optimum allocation of investment.

Thus, it can be stated that in western type economies the stock exchange was one of the institutions resulting from the long process of institutionalisation of various forms of entrepreneurship. Stock exchanges in these economies developed as an important institution for industrial financing and community's saving and investment activity. The London Stock Exchange is the world's oldest stock exchange, formally organised on 15th July, 1730. It is also worth mentioning that over a long period of time in some major industrially developed economies like that of USA and Japan, due to their large size, a number of corporations became so influential and dominant that the debate, relating to whether these corporations are subordinate to macroeconomic factors or they are in position to influence them, became increasingly significant.[5]

1.1.2 Stock Exchanges in India

A stock exchange is the place where securities, shares, debentures and bonds of joint stock companies, central and state governments, local bodies and foreign governments are bought and sold. It is the nerve center of capital market. Changes in the capital market are brought about by a complex set of factors, operating in the market simultaneously. Such changes are subject to secular trends set by the economic progress of the nation and governed by the factors like general economic situation, financial and monetary policies, tax changes, political environment, international, economic and financial development and so on.

Stock exchanges in India have been defined under Section 2(i) of Securities Contract Regulation Act, 1956 as a "body of individuals whether incorporated or not, constituted for the purpose of assisting, regulating or controlling the business of buying, selling or dealing in securities".

Stock exchanges are usually formed as association of persons or companies under section 25 of the Companies Act, 1956. In earlier days, stock exchanges were formed with the charitable objectives. However, that era has come to an end and presently more and more stock exchanges are formed with profit-making objectives. Moreover, with recent developments in Securities Contract Regulation Act, 1956 (SCRA, 1956) all stock exchanges which were not corporatised have been asked to corporatise, through an ordinance on corporatisation and demutualization.[6] Thus the structure of the stock exchanges have undergone a change after fully implementation of demutualization scheme (segregation of ownership from management and trading).

A stock exchange thus provides necessary mobility to capital and directs the flow of capital into profitable and successful enterprises.

In other words, stock exchange is a market place like any other centralized market where both buyers and sellers come and conduct their business of purchase and sale of shares and securities. It is a market place for shares and securities where trading takes place in a controlled and protected environment.

In India only recognized stock exchanges can operate. The recognition is governed under the provisions of Securities Contract Regulation Act, 1956 (SCRA, 1956). Securities and Exchange Board of India (SEBI) is the monitoring and regulatory authority of stock markets in India. There were 19 recognized stock exchanges in India by the end of the year 2008. Mangalore Stock Exchange was derecognized by SEBI in the year 2006 while Magadh, Hyderabad and Saurashtra Kutch Stock Exchanges were derecognized in the year 2007.

1.1.3 Growth of Stock Exchanges in India

(a) Pre-Independence

Indian stock exchanges or markets are one of the oldest in Asia. Its history dates back to nearly 200 years ago. The earliest records of security dealings in India are scanty and obscure. The East India Company was the dominant institution in those days and business in its loan securities used to be transacted towards the close of the eighteenth century. By 1830's, business on corporate stocks and shares in Bank and Cotton Presses took place in Bombay. Though the trading list was broader in 1839, there were only half a dozen brokers recognized by banks and merchants during the period 1840-50. The 1850's witnessed a rapid development of commercial enterprises and brokerage business attracted many individuals to the field and by 1860 the number of brokers increased to 60.[7]

With the passage of time and the implementation of Joint Stock Companies Act in 1850, the number of companies involved in various types of trades started growing at a faster pace. Since India at that time was a colony of the British empire, important policy decisions pertaining to the Indian economy were either taken or influenced by the Empire. Therefore, most of the decisions aimed at protecting the interest of British manufacturing and service industry. Although Britishers advocated the policy of free trade, in actual British interest exploited Indian industry through unequal trade by making India a hinterland for the production and sale of raw materials and purchase of manufactured goods from United Kingdom.[8]

In 1860-61 the American Civil War broke out and cotton supply from United States was stopped. Thus, the 'Share Mania' in India begun. The number of brokers increased to about 200 to 250. However, at the end of the American Civil War, in 1865, a disastrous slump began. For instance, Bank of Bombay Share which had touched Rs. 2850 could only be sold at Rs. 87. At the end of the American Civil War, the brokers who thrived out of Civil War in 1874 found a place in a street (presently known as Dalal Street) where they would conveniently assemble and transact business. It was in the year 1875 that BSE was established as the "Native Share and Stock Brokers' Association". In 1895, the stock exchange acquired a premise in the same street and it was inaugurated in 1899. Thus, the stock exchange at Bombay was consolidated.

Ahmedabad gained importance next to Bombay with respect to cotton textile industry. After 1880, many mills originated from Ahmedabad and rapidly forged ahead. As new mills were floated, the need for a Stock Exchange at Ahmedabad was realized and in 1894 the brokers formed "The Ahmedabad Share and Stock Brokers' Association". What the cotton textile industry was to Bombay and Ahmedabad, the jute industry was to Calcutta. Also tea and coal industries were the other major industrial groups in Calcutta.

After the Share Mania in 1861-65 and in the 1870's there was a sharp boom in jute shares, which was followed by a boom in tea shares in the 1880's and 1890's; and a coal boom between 1904 and 1908. On June 1908, some leading brokers formed "The Calcutta Stock Exchange Association". In the beginning of the twentieth century, the industrial revolution was on the way in India with the Swadeshi Movement; and with the inauguration of the Tata Iron and Steel Company Limited in 1907, an important stage in industrial advancement under Indian enterprise was reached. In 1920, the then demure city of Madras had the maiden thrill of a stock exchange functioning in its midst, under the name and style of "The Madras Stock Exchange" with 100 members.

However, when boom faded, the number of members stood reduced from 100 to 3, by 1923, and so it went out of existence. In 1935, the stock market activity improved, especially in South India where there was a rapid increase in the number of textile mills and many plantation companies were floated. In 1937, a stock exchange was once again organized in Madras, Madras Stock Exchange Association (Pvt.) Limited. (In 1957, the name was changed to Madras Stock Exchange Limited). Lahore Stock Exchange was formed in 1934 and it had a brief life. It was merged with the Punjab Stock Exchange Limited, which was incorporated in 1936.

The Second World War broke out in 1939. It gave a sharp boom, which was followed by a slump. But, in 1943, the situation changed radically, when India was fully mobilized as a supply base. On account of the restrictive controls on cotton, bullion, seeds and other commodities, those dealing in them found the stock market as the only outlet for their activities. They were anxious to join the trade and their number was swelled by numerous others. Many stock exchanges, The Uttar Pradesh Stock Exchange Limited (1940), Nagpur Stock Exchange Limited (1940) and Hyderabad Stock Exchange Limited (1944) were floated. In Delhi two stock exchanges—Delhi Stock and Share Brokers' Association Limited and the Delhi Stocks and Share Exchange Limited were floated and later in June 1947, amalgamated into the Delhi Stock Exchange Association Limited.

(b) Post-Independence

Most of the stock exchanges languished till 1957 when they applied to the Central Government for recognition under the Securities Contracts (Regulation) Act, 1956. Only Bombay, Calcutta, Madras, Ahmedabad, Delhi, Hyderabad and Indore, the well-established exchanges were recognized under the Act. Some of the members of other associations were required to be admitted by the recognized stock exchanges on a concessional basis, but acting on the principle of unitary control, all these pseudo stock exchanges were refused recognition by the Government of India and they thereupon ceased to function. Thus, during sixties there were seven recognized stock exchanges in India. The number virtually remained unchanged, for nearly two decades.

New developments took place in the Indian economy during eighties. Economic Liberalisation can be termed as a point of departure insofar as the economic policy is concerned. The new economic policy encompassed wide ranging measures such as delicensing of a number of industries, throwing open to the private sector a number of industries reserved for the public sector, the lowering of personal and corporate tax rates, raising of the interest rate on convertible debentures of companies, raising the asset limit for applicability of Monopolies and Restrictive Trade Practices (MRTP) Act, bringing in more items under open general licence (OGL), liberal approach in regard to foreign collaborations, allowing scope for dominant undertakings to go in for diversification projects. The liberalisation also included special incentives for private enterprise by way of reduction in direct taxes and tax free high yielding instruments without any financial limit on individual subscription.[9]

The company finance studies by the Reserve Bank of India reveal that the proportion of the private corporate sector's internal sources to its total resources of funds has been declining over the years.[10] A sharp increase in the number of public limited companies in private corporate sector can also be viewed in the context of the company law provisions that allowed public limited companies to raise money from public.[11] During 1980-90 period an increase of

132 per cent in the number of public limited companies was registered as compared to an increase of only 38 per cent during the decade 1970-80.[12] With liberalisation and increased demand for funds on the part of private corporate sector, investment in shares and debentures became middle class phenomenon.[13] Further tax and other benefits associated with the investment in corporate securities attracted the salaried middle class and non-resident Indian investors.[14]

In consonance with new economic policy, during the decade of eighties, a number of new stock exchanges were established. These are :

- Cochin Stock Exchange (1980),
- Uttar Pradesh Stock Exchange Association Limited (at Kanpur, 1982),
- Pune Stock Exchange Limited (1982),
- Ludhiana Stock Exchange Association Limited (1983),
- Gauhati Stock Exchange Limited (1984),
- Kanara Stock Exchange Limited (at Mangalore, 1985),
- Magadh Stock Exchange Association (at Patna, 1986),
- Jaipur Stock Exchange Limited (1989),
- Bhubaneswar Stock Exchange Association Limited (1989),
- Saurashtra Kutch Stock Exchange Limited (at Rajkot, 1989), and
- Vadodara Stock Exchange Limited (at Baroda, 1990).

With the formation of Over The Counter Stock Exchange of India and the emergence of National Stock Exchange in the year 2004, the number of stock exchanges increased to 23 by the year 2000. At present, there are 19 stock exchanges recognized by the Central Government and Securities and Exchange Board of India. A list of the recognized stock exchanges is given in Annexure I-A.

The securities market in India has essentially three categories of participants, viz., the issuer of securities, the investors in the securities and the intermediaries. The issuers are the borrowers or deficit savers, who issue securities to raise funds. The investors, who are surplus savers, deploy their savings by subscribing to these securities. The intermediaries are the agents who match the needs of users and suppliers of funds for a commission. These intermediaries function to help both the issuers and investors to achieve their respective goals. There are large variety and number of intermediaries providing various services in the Indian securities market. (Table 1.1).

The securities market has two interdependent and inseparable segments, the new issues (primary) market and the stock (secondary) market. The primary market provides the channel for creation and sale of new securities, while the secondary market deals in securities previously issued.

The securities issued in the primary market are issued by public limited companies or by government agencies. The resources in this kind of market are mobilized either through the public issue or through private placement route. It is a public issue if anybody and everybody can subscribe for it, whereas if the issue is made available to a selected group of persons it is termed as private placement. There are two major types of issuers of securities, the corporate entities who issue mainly debt and equity instruments and the government (central as well as state) who issue debt securities (dated securities and treasury bills).

The secondary market enables participants who hold securities to adjust their holdings in response to changes in their assessment of risks and returns. Once the new securities are issued in the primary market they are traded in the stock (secondary) market. The secondary market operates through two mediums, namely, the over-the-counter (OTC) market and the exchange-traded market. OTC markets are informal markets where trades are negotiated. Most of the trades in the government securities are in the OTC market. All the spot trades where securities are traded for immediate delivery and payment take place in the OTC market. The other option is to trade using the infrastructure provided by the stock exchanges. The exchanges in India follow a systematic settlement period. All the trades taking place over a trading cycle (day=T) are settled together after a certain time (T+2 day). The trades executed on exchanges are cleared and settled by a clearing corporation. The clearing corporation acts as a counterparty and guarantees settlement. A variant of the secondary market is the forward market, where securities are traded for future delivery and payment. A variant of the forward market is Futures and Options market. Presently, only two exchanges viz., National Stock Exchange of India Ltd. (NSE) and Bombay Stock Exchange (BSE) provides trading in the Futures and Options.

A perusal of the Table 1.1 reveals that the number of stock exchanges declined from 23 in the year 2000 to 19 by the end of the financial year 2008. Two stock exchanges, namely, NSE and BSE are active players in the derivatives market.

The stock exchanges have a total number of 9487 registered brokers. Out of these 4190 registered corporate brokers.

At the end of the financial year 2008 there were 44074 sub brokers and 1442 are derivative brokers working in these exchanges. There are two depositories, i.e. National Securities Depository Limited (NSDL) and Central Depository Service Limited (CDSL) and the depository participants increased from 191 in 2000 to 654 in year 2008. The number of merchant bankers have, however, decreased from 186 in the year 2000 to 155 in the year 2008.

There were total 1319 registered foreign institutional investors by the end of the year 2008. The number increased by 161% from the year 2001 when the number was only 506. This increase shows the strengths and depth of Indian capital markets and confidence reposed in the growing economy by the foreign players. There were 50 bankers to an issue by the end of the year 2008. The number of underwriters has decreased from 42 in the year 2000 to 35 by the end of the year 2008. The number of debenture trustees has also decreased from 38 in the year 2000 to 28 in the year 2008. There are 5 credit rating agencies in India by the year 2008.

However, there has been a considerably growth in the number of venture capital funds which were nil in the year 2000 and are now 106 in the year 2008. Similarly, foreign

TABLE 1.1

Market Participants in Capital Markets

Market Intermediaries	*As on 31st March*								
	2000	2001	2002	2003	2004	2005	2006	2007	2008
Stock Exchanges (Cash Market)	23	23	23	23	23	22	22	21	19
Stock Exchanges (Derivatives Market)	2	2	2	2	2	2	2	2	2
Brokers (Cash Segment)	9192	9782	9687	9519	9368	9128	9335	9443	9487
Corporate Brokers (Cash Segment)	3316	3808	3862	3835	3787	3773	3961	4110	4190
Sub-Brokers (Cash Segment)	5675	9957	12208	13291	12815	13684	23479	27541	44074
Brokers (Derivatives)	NA	519	705	795	829	994	1120	1258	1442
Foreign Institutional Investors	506	527	490	502	540	685	882	997	1319
Custodian	15	14	12	11	11	11	11	11	15
Depositories	2	2	2	2	2	2	2	2	2
Depository Participants	191	335	380	438	431	477	526	593	654
Merchant Bankers	186	233	145	124	123	128	130	152	155
Bankers to an issue	68	69	68	67	55	59	60	47	50

Underwriters	42	57	54	43	47	59	57	45	35
Debenture Trustees	38	37	40	35	34	35	32	30	28
Credit Rating Agencies	4	4	4	4	4	4	4	4	5
Venture Capital Funds	---	35	34	43	45	50	80	90	106
Foreign Venture Capital Investors	---	1	2	6	9	14	39	78	97
Registrars to an issue and Share transfer Agent	242	186	161	143	78	83	83	82	76
Portfolio Managers	23	39	47	54	60	84	132	158	205
Mutual Funds	38	39	38	38	37	39	38	40	40

Source: http://www.sebi.gov.in/Index.jsp (assessed on 5th May, 2009).

investor venture capital has shown remarkable interest in the market and their number has increased from nil in the year 2000 to 97 in the year 2008. The number of registrars to an issue and share transfer agents has decreased from 242 in the year 2000 to 76 by the year 2008. The number of portfolio managers has shown tremendous increase from 23 in the year 2000 to 205 by the end of the year 2008. The number of mutual funds has shown steady growth from 38 in the year 2000 to 40 by the year 2008.

Growth in turnover of various stock exchanges in India during the period 2001-02 to 2007-08 is given in the Table 1.2. The turnover consists of Cash Market (CM) transactions, Wholesale Debt Market (WDM) transactions and Futures and Options (F&O) market transactions. The NSE and BSE stick exchanges have all the three categories of transactions included in turnover whereas the turnover of all other regional exchanges consists only of cash market transaction.

The table clearly brings out that the increase in turnover took place mostly at the bigger stock exchanges.

The National Stock Exchange stands as the market leader with 90.27 per cent of total turnover by end of the year 2007-08. Top two stock exchanges, namely, NSE and BSE account for 99.99 per cent of the total turnover of all the stock exchanges taken together, while the rest 19 stock exchanges had negligible volumes during 2007-08. It needs to be mentioned here that the four stock exchanges derecognized by SEBI are Magadh, Mangalore, Hyderabad and Saurashtra Kutch.

The exchange-wise distribution of brokers for the years 2000 through 2008 is given in Tables 1.3(a), 1.3(b) and 1.3(c).

A further look into the Tables 1.3(a), 1.3(b) and 1.3(c) shows that there were total 991 registered brokers on National Stock Exchange in the year 1999-2000. Out of which 86.9 per cent were corporate brokers in the NSE and the number increased to 1129 by the year 2007-08. Out of these 92 per cent were corporate brokers. Similarly in the case of BSE the number of brokers was 631 in the year 1999-2000, having 61 per cent corporate brokers. The number increased to 946 in the year 2008. Further out of these (946) 81.1 per cent are corporate brokers. Similarly in OTCEI the number of

TABLE 1.2

Growth in Turnover* of Stock Exchanges in India

Sr. No.	Stock Exchanges	2001-02 (Rs. Mn)	2002-03 (Rs. Mn)	2003-04 (Rs. Mn)	2004-05 (Rs. Mn)	2005-06 (Rs. Mn)	2006-07 (Rs. Mn)	2007-08 (Rs. Mn)
1	2	3	4	5	6	7	8	9
1.	NSE	15,622,830 (80.24)	21,265,445 (85.74	45,462,793 (89.50)	45,744,186 (89.37)	68,693,315 (89.32)	95,206,640 (90.33)	169,238,329 (90.27)
2.	BSE	3,093,156 (15.88)	3,165,516 (12.76)	5,146,730 (10.13)	5,357,913 (10.46)	8,160,830 (10.61)	10,167,917 (9.64)	18,233,239 (9.72)
3.	Calcutta	270,747 (1.39)	65,399 (0.26)	19,275 (0.03)	27,150 (0.05)	28,000 (0.03)	6,940 (0.00)	4,460 (0.00)
4.	Delhi	58,280 (0.29)	111 (0.00)	34 (0.00)	0	0	0	0
5.	Ahmedabad	148,435 (0.76)	154,586 (0.62)	45,445 (0.08)	80 (0.00)	0	0	0
6.	Uttar Pradesh	252,373 (1.29)	147,634 (0.59)	117,510 (0.23)	53,430 (0.10)	14,860 (0.01)	7,990 (0.00)	4,750 (0.00)
7.	Ludhiana	8,566 (0.04)	0	0	0	0	0	0
8.	Pune	11,710 (0.06)	18 (0.00)	0	3 (0.00)	0	0	0
9.	Bangalore	703 (0.00)	0	1 (0.00)	0	0	0	0
10.	Hyderabad**	413 (0.00)	46 (0.00)	20 (0.00)	140 (0.00)	890 (0.00)	920 (0.00)	0
11.	ICSE/ISE	554 (0.00)	648 (0.00)	1 (0.00)	0	0	0	0

(Contd.)

TABLE 1.2 (*Contd.*)

1	2	3	4	5	6	7	8	9
12.	Cochin	0	0	0	0	0	0	0
13.	OTCEI	38 (0.00)	1 (0.00)	158 (0.00)	0	0.1 (0.00)	0	0
14.	Madras	241 (0.00)	0	1,009 (0.00)	270 (0.00)	50 (0.00)	12 (0.00)	0
15.	Madhya Pradesh	235 (0.00)	0	0	0	0	0	0
16.	Magadh**	0	5 (0.00)	1 (0.00)	0	910 (0.00)	0	0
17.	Vadodara	101 (0.00)	25 (0.00)	1 (0.00)	0	0	0	0
18.	Gauhati	1 (0.00)	1 (0.00)	0	0	0	0	0
19.	Bhubaneswar	0	0	0	0	0	0	0
20.	Coimbatore	266 (0.00)	0	0	0	0	0	0
21.	Jaipur	0	0	0	0	0	0	0
22.	SKSE**	0	0	0	0	0	0	0
23.	Mangalore**	0	0	0	0	0	0	0
	Total	19,468,650 (100)	24,799,434 (100)	50,792,977 (100)	51,183,172 (100)	76,898,855 (100)	105,390,419 (100)	187,480,780 (100)

Figures in parenthesis are per centages.
*Turnover means total value of transactions of securities in all market segments of an Exchange. For NSE and BSE all three segments viz., Cash Market, Futures and Options and Wholesale Debt Market are included.
**4 Stock Exchanges have been derecognized by SEBI.
Source: http://www.sebi.gov.in/Index.jsp (assessed on 10th May, 2009)

TABLE I.3(a)

Exchange-wise Number of Brokers

Stock Exchange	*1999-00*			*2000-01*			*2001-02*		
	Total Brokers	*Corporate Brokers*	*Corporate Brokers as a percent of total brokers*	*Total Brokers*	*Corporate Brokers*	*Corporate Brokers as a percent of total brokers*	*Total Brokers*	*Corporate Brokers*	*Corporate Brokers as a percent of total brokers*
1	*2*	*3*	*4*	*5*	*6*	*7*	*8*	*9*	*10*
Ahmedabad	301	118	39.2	326	144	44.2	325	151	46.5
Bangalore	241	103	42.7	249	110	44.2	249	112	45
BSE	631	385	61	689	463	67.2	660	463	70.2
Delhi	234	15	6.4	234	17	7.3	232	17	7.3
Calcutta	949	159	16.8	993	203	20.4	992	205	20.7
Cochin	491	67	13.6	492	71	14.4	470	74	15.7
Coimbatore	198	62	31.3	197	62	31.5	193	63	32.6
Delhi	392	201	51.3	393	215	54.7	379	214	56.5
Gauhati	206	5	2.4	193	5	2.6	194	5	2.6
Hyderabad	310	102	32.9	310	114	36.8	303	117	38.6
ICSE	269	100	37.2	595	230	38.7	630	245	38.9

(Contd.)

TABLE I.3(a) *(Contd.)*

1	*2*	*3*	*4*	*5*	*6*	*7*	*8*	*9*	*10*
Jaipur	593	16	2.7	595	17	2.9	592	21	3.6
Ludhiana	284	70	24.6	302	79	26.2	300	83	27.7
Madhya Pradesh	187	28	15	187	34	18.2	187	34	18.2
Madras	200	67	33.5	202	71	35.1	192	71	37
Magadh	199	15	7.5	204	19	9.3	200	19	9.5
Ahmedabad	146	14	9.6	139	14	10.1	138	15	10.9
NSE	991	861	86.9	1074	947	88.2	1065	940	88.3
OTCEI	890	668	75.1	896	694	77.5	902	705	78.2
Pune	200	45	22.5	201	56	27.9	196	60	30.6
Saurashtra Kutch	445	64	14.4	448	78	17.4	446	82	18.4
UPSEV	514	86	16.7	541	100	18.3	520	101	19.4
Vadodara	321	65	20.2	322	65	20.2	322	65	20.2
Total	9192	3316	36.1	9782	3808	38.9	9687	3862	39.9

Source: http://www.sebi.gov.in/Index.jsp (assessed on 10th May, 2009).

TABLE I.3(b)

Exchange-eise Number of Brokers

Stock Exchange	1999-00			2000-01			2001-02		
	Total Brokers	Corporate Brokers	Corporate Brokers as a per-cent of total brokers	Total Brokers	Corporate Brokers	Corporate Brokers as a per-cent of total brokers	Total Brokers	Corporate Brokers	Corporate Brokers as a per-cent of total brokers
1	2	3	4	5	6	7	8	9	10
Ahmedabad	323	152	47.1	323	152	47.1	317	150	47.3
Bangalore	245	114	46.5	242	116	47.9	250	119	47.6
BSE	665	468	70.4	673	479	71.2	726	534	73.6
Delhi	233	18	7.7	229	18	7.9	221	18	8.1
Calcutta	987	201	20.4	980	200	20.4	962	204	21.2
Cochin	464	75	16.2	468	82	17.5	446	76	17
Coimbatore	182	62	34.1	177	61	34.5	135	49	36.3
Delhi	374	213	57	373	215	57.6	376	215	57.2
Gauhati	175	5	2.9	172	5	2.9	119	4	3.4

(Contd.)

TABLE 1.3(b) *(Contd.)*

1	2	3	4	5	6	7	8	9	10
Hyderabad	306	120	39.2	305	119	39	288	118	41
ICSE	630	247	39.2	633	248	39.2	654	250	38.2
Jaipur	555	19	3.4	532	19	3.6	522	19	3.6
Ludhiana	302	85	28.1	297	85	28.6	293	84	28.7
Madhya Pradesh	188	34	18.1	179	35	19.6	174	35	20.1
Madras	186	71	38.2	182	70	38.5	178	69	38.8
Magadh	199	20	10.1	195	22	11.3	198	22	11.1
Ahmedabad	116	11	9.5	105	10	9.5	66	9	13.6
NSE	1036	918	88.6	970	863	89	976	877	89.9
OTCEI	883	690	78.1	867	675	77.9	801	616	76.9
Pune	197	59	29.9	197	59	29.9	186	55	29.6
Saurashtra Kutch	436	85	19.5	437	86	19.7	425	83	19.5
UPSEV	518	3	19.9	514	104	20.2	504	103	20.4
Vadodara	319	65	20.4	318	64	20.1	311	64	20.6
Total	9519	3835	40.3	9368	3787	40.4	9128	3773	41.3

Source: http://www.sebi.gov.in/Index.jsp (assessed on 10th May, 2009).

TABLE I.3(c)

Exchange-wise Number of Brokers

Stock Exchange	1999-00			2000-01			2001-02		
	Total Brokers	Corporate Brokers	Corporate Brokers as a per-cent of total brokers	Total Brokers	Corporate Brokers	Corporate Brokers as a per-cent of total brokers	Total Brokers	Corporate Brokers	Corporate Brokers as a per-cent of total brokers
1	*2*	*3*	*4*	*5*	*6*	*7*	*8*	*9*	*10*
Ahmedabad	317	152	48	317	153	48.3	321	157	48.9
Bangalore	256	125	48.8	256	125	48.8	256	124	48.4
BSE	840	661	78.7	901	722	80.1	946	767	81.1
Delhi	219	19	8.7	216	19	8.8	214	19	8.9
Calcutta	962	204	21.2	960	204	21.3	957	204	21.3
Cochin	434	79	18.2	432	80	18.5	435	80	18.4
Coimbatore	135	48	35.6	135	48	35.6	135	48	35.6
Delhi	375	214	57.1	374	213	57	374	213	57
Gauhati	110	4	3.6	104	3	2.9	103	3	2.9
Hyderabad	304	122	40.1	304	122	40.1	304	122	40.1
ICSE	788	283	35.9	925	336	36.3	935	345	36.9

(Contd.)

TABLE 1.3(c)

1	2	3	4	5	6	7	8	9	'10
Jaipur	507	19	3.8	492	18	3.7	488	18	3.7
Ludhiana	293	86	29.4	293	85	29	297	85	28.6
Madhya Pradesh	174	35	20.1	174	35	20.1	174	34	19.5
Madras	182	71	39	181	71	39.2	181	71	39.2
Magadh	198	22	11.1	197	22	11.2	197	22	11.2
Ahmedabad	66	9	13.6	59	9	15.3	59	9	15.3
NSE	1014	922	90.9	1077	988	91.7	1129	1039	92
OTCEI	769	588	76.5	752	574	76.3	719	551	76.6
Pune	192	57	29.7	188	55	29.3	188	55	29.3
Saurashtra Kutch	426	84	19.7	411	82	20	410	82	20
UPSEV	463	93	20.1	384	82	21.4	354	78	22
Vadodara	311	64	20.6	311	64	20.6	311	64	20.6
Total	9335	3961	42.4	443	4110	43.5	9487	4190	44.2

Source: http://www.sebi.gov.in/Index.jsp (assessed on 10th May, 2009).

brokers were 890 in the year 2000 out of which 75.1 per cent are corporate brokers, however by the year 2008 the number of brokers decreased to 719 in OTCEI but this has resulted in marginal increase of corporate brokers to 76.6 per cent.

The tables further reveal that in some of the other prominent regional exchanges like Delhi Stock Exchange the number of registered brokers was 392 in the year 2000 out of which 51.3 per cent are corporate brokers and by the end of the year 2008 the number of brokers decreased to 214 with a fall in per centage of corporate brokers to merely 8.9 per cent. The Calcutta Stock Exchange has 949 registered brokers in the year 2000 out of which 16.8 per cent are corporate brokers and by the end of the year 2008 the number of registered brokers are 957 including 21.3 per cent of corporate brokers. Similarly in Ludhiana there are 284 brokers in the year 2000 out of which 24.6 per cent are corporate brokers and by the end of the year 2008 the number increased to 297 out of which 28.6 per cent are corporate brokers. In Jaipur Stock Exchange the number of registered brokers are 593 including 2.7 per cent as corporate brokers in the year 2000 and by the year 2008 it decreased to 488 out of which 3.7 per cent are the corporate brokers.

It may be concluded that the number of registered brokers on the stock exchanges in India increased from 9192 in the year 2000 to 9487 by the end of the year 2008.

1.1.4 Regional Stock Exchanges in India

The Indian economic scene has undergone a metamorphosis in the last decade of 20th century. The major driving factor behind the same has been the impact of globalization, liberalization and privatization taking place not only in the country but also globally with its attendant effects. One can see major structural changes in India, the most striking being those in the Indian capital market. Earlier, marked by numerous thriving regional bourses, which were the vehicles of earning and ease for the investors, the capital market today stands with a few proud stock exchanges with a nationwide reach such as National Stock Exchange (NSE) and Bombay Stock Exchange (BSE). The turnover of old buddies has dwindled, their working reduced to a stillness and they are on the brink of a miserable farewell from the capital market campus.

Regional Stock Exchanges perform very important functions in the economy. They not only act as catalyst for channelising the savings of the individuals or private sector but also act as barometer of the economy, indicating the financial health of the economy. Some of the important functions performed by the stock exchanges are briefly discussed below:

(a) Raising capital for businesses

The stock exchanges provides companies with the facility to raise capital for expansion through selling shares to the investing public.

The functioning of the stock exchange has therefore to be such as to create a climate conducive to an active primary market (new issues market) and to ensure fair and efficient trading in securities in the secondary market (stock exchange) and to establish a harmonious relationship between the two.[15]

In other words, the institution of stock exchange is expected to facilitate the channelisation of savings especially from the household sector to meet the investment requirements of the productive sectors of the economy primarily by ensuring a market place, that provides liquidity to capital market instruments through fair and transparent trading practices.[16]

The responsibility therefore to ensure the 'harmonious relationship' between new issues market and secondary market or stock exchange rests with the functioning of stock exchanges.

(b) Mobilizing savings for investment

The stock exchanges by providing support to the primary market assist in mobilization of savings of individuals. When people draw their savings and invest in shares, it leads to a more rational allocation of resources because funds, which could have been consumed, or kept in idle deposits with banks, are mobilized and redirected to promote business activity with benefits for several economic sectors such as agriculture, commerce and industry, resulting in a stronger economic growth and higher productivity levels and firms.

(c) Facilitating company growth

Companies view acquisitions as an opportunity to expand product lines, increase distribution channels,. hedge against volatility, increase its market share, or acquire other necessary business assets. A takeover bid or a merger agreement through the stock market is one of the simplest and most common ways for a company to grow by acquisition or fusion.

(d) Redistribution of wealth

Stocks exchanges do not exist to redistribute wealth. However, both casual and professional stock investors, through dividends and stock price increases that may result in capital gains, will share in the wealth of profitable businesses.

(e) Corporate governance

By having a wide and varied scope of owners, companies generally tend to improve on their management standards and efficiency in order to satisfy the demands of these shareholders and the more stringent rules for public corporations imposed by public stock exchanges and the government. Consequently, it is alleged that public companies (companies that are owned by shareholders who are members of the general public and trade shares on public exchanges) tend to have better management records than privately-held companies (those companies where shares are not publicly traded, often owned by the company founders and/or their families and heirs, or otherwise by a small group of investors). However, some well documented cases are known where it is alleged that there has been considerable slippage in corporate governance on the part of some public companies, Pets.com (2000), Enron Corporation (2001), One.Tel (2001), Sunbeam (2001), Webvan (2001), Adelphia (2002), MCI WorldCom (2002), or Parmalat (2003), are among the most widely scrutinized by the media) and latest being the Indian IT major Satyam (2008).

(f) Creating investment opportunities for small investors

As opposed to other businesses that require huge capital outlay, investing in shares is open to both the large and small stock investors because a person buys the number of shares they can afford. Therefore, the stock exchange provides the opportunity for small investors to own shares of the same companies as large investors.

(g) Government capital-raising for development projects

Governments at various levels may decide to borrow money in order to finance infrastructure projects such as sewage and water treatment works or housing estates by selling another category of securities known as bonds. These bonds can be raised through the stock exchange whereby members of the public buy them, thus loaning money to the government. The issuance of such bonds can obviate the need to directly tax the citizens in order to finance development, although by securing such bonds with the full faith and credit of the government instead of with collateral, the result is that the government must tax the citizens or otherwise raise additional funds to make any regular coupon payments and refund the principal when the bonds mature.

(h) Barometer of the economy

At the stock exchange, share prices rise and fall depending, largely, on market forces. Share prices tend to rise or remain stable when companies and the economy in general show signs of stability and growth. An economic recession, depression, or financial crisis could eventually lead to a stock market crash. Therefore, the movement of share prices and in general of the stock indexes can be an indicator of the general trend in the economy.

1.1.5 Problems and Prospects of RSEs

(a) Problems

The problems which are faced by the regional exchanges are numerous. It is beyond the scope of the present study to comment on each of these problems in detail. They range from the formation of National Stock

Exchange, Shift in investors' preference towards screen-based trading and technology, doing away of mandatory listing requirement clause of regional companies by the regulator to unsupportive role of regulatory authority. These problems are discussed below:

1. The decision of the SEBI in 1994-95 to set-up the NSE on national basis, has finished the concept of the regional stock exchanges. SEBI allowed the NSE to have its terminals in all the cities across the country. Further the BSE was also allowed to go anywhere in the country, with the result that the regional stock exchanges received a severe setback in business volumes.
2. Trading technology is getting more complex and investors are tending to gravitate to the larger exchanges because of better rates and higher liquidity. Regional exchanges have experienced negative growth in trading volumes in 1996-97. The Hyderabad Stock Exchange, for example, saw a 62 per cent fall in volumes in 1996-97 over 1995-96. Also, Rs. 150 crore spent on computerization of RSEs has gone waste due to bottom shooting trading volumes.
3. Doing away with the compulsory listing clause of regional companies at RSEs sounded the death knell for regional stock exchanges, which were already reeling under the impact of computerized nationwide trading. Regional stock exchanges had been able to build up a traded list of securities mostly on the basis of the compulsory listing clause. It was mandatory for all corporates, which had issued shares to the public, to list their shares in the major regional stock exchange in the region where it was registered.
4. The Kania Committee (March 2002) on corporatisation and demutualization, appointed by SEBI, strongly recommended the abolition of the concept of regional stock exchanges in the country. The committee was of the opinion that the concept

of regional stock exchanges, which was introduced in the days of manual trading and open outcry system to encourage mobilization of resources and development of equity cult in the country, has lost relevance in the days of automated trading. Interestingly, the recommendations of the committee are at variance with the position taken by the then SEBI Chairman, Mr. G.N. Bajpai.

5. Financial position of the regional stock exchanges deteriorated on account of non-payment of regular listing fee. Ludhiana Stock Exchange had as many as 455 listed companies and the annual recovery of listing fee was of the order Rs. 1.30 crore, but the actual recovery was only Rs. 90 lakh in the year 2000. As earlier stated a sum of Rs. 150 crore spent by the regional stock exchanges in the country on computerization has been wasted, as the same facility was never optimally utilized. Moreover, RSEs did not had the muscle to compete with financial strength of large exchanges.
6. SEBI, which regulates and controls the functioning of capital markets and stock exchanges in India has not shown much concern for the fate of RSEs. The big players have been the apple of its eyes and its regulations biased for their fortune.

(b) Prospects

Due to the rapid expansion of the National and Bombay stock exchanges into small centers and cities, regional exchanges struggled to survive. Good quality stocks vanished from the bourses. Barely 500 of the 6,000 plus scripts listed on the bourses are actively traded on any trading day. With almost all the RSEs considered clinically dead, following the abolition of 'badla' and the introduction of compulsory rolling settlement from July 2001, the market regulator has suggested two alternatives for the RSEs. Firstly, providing exit route to the RSEs from equities trading to enable them to take up other financial market activities. Secondly, revive them through consolidation, mergers and takeovers. The second alternative is learnt to have gained more support following the study of the successful model of consolidation for the stock exchanges adopted in Europe, through which the exchanges located in Paris, Brussels and Amsterdam merged into a single entity. The expert committee has suggested setting up of Indonext, a third National Stock Exchange, similar to the Euronext by merging regional stock exchanges. This will help utilize the infrastructure of regional stock exchanges. The trading system of the new exchange would be centralized at the location of any of the participating exchanges. If SEBI prefers to adopt this model for the revival of RSEs, as many as 4,500 member brokers of these stock exchanges would get automatic trading right on single trading floor, which would result in increased depth and width of the market for small and mid cap scrips. However, in the absence of concrete solution the regional stock exchanges are confronting a dark future.

1.1.6 Reforms in Indian Capital Markets

During the last decade, there have been substantial regulatory, structural, institutional and operational changes in the securities industry. These have been brought in with the objective of improving market efficiency, enhancing transparency, preventing unfair trade practices and bringing the Indian market up to the international standards. The following paragraphs list the principal reform measures undertaken since 1992.

(a) SEBI Act, 1992

It created the securities market regulator, the SEBI, with the main objective and responsibility for (a) protecting the interests of investors in securities, (b) promoting the development of the securities market, and (c) regulating the securities market. Its regulatory jurisdiction extends over corporate in the issuance of capital and transfer of securities, in addition to all intermediaries and persons associated with securities market. The courts have upheld the powers of SEBI to impose monetary penalties and to levy fees from market intermediaries.

Enactment of the SEBI Act was the first attempt towards integrated regulation of the securities market. SEBI was given full authority and jurisdiction over the securities market under the Act, and was given concurrent/delegated powers for various provisions under the Companies Act and the SCRA.

(b) DIP Guidelines

With the repeal of the Capital Issues (Control) Act, 1947 in May 1992, Government's control over issue of capital, pricing of the issues, fixing of premia and rates of interest on debentures, etc. ceased. Thereafter, the market has been allowed to allocate resources among the competing uses. In the interest of investors, SEBI issued the Disclosure and Investor Protection (DIP) guidelines. These guidelines contain a substantial body of requirements for issuers/intermediaries, with a broad intention to ensure that all the concerned entities observe high standards of integrity and fair dealing.

The guidelines cast a responsibility on the lead managers to issue a due diligence certificate, stating that they have examined the prospectus and that it brings out all the facts and does not contain anything wrong or misleading. Issuers are now required to comply with the guidelines and then access the market. The companies can access the market only if they fulfil minimum eligibility norms in terms of their track record of distributable profits and net worth.

(c) Screen-based Trading

Prior to setting up of NSE, the trading on stock exchanges in India used to take place through an open outcry system. This system did not allow immediate matching or recording of trades. This was time consuming and imposed limits on trading. In order to provide efficiency, liquidity and transparency, NSE introduced a nation-wide on-line fully-automated screen-based trading system (SBTS). In this system a member can punch into the computer, quantities of securities and the prices at which he desires to transact and the transaction is executed as soon as it finds a matching sale or buy order from a counter-party. It allows a large number of participants, irrespective of their geographical locations, to trade with one another simultaneously, improving the depth and liquidity of the market. Given the efficiency and cost effectiveness delivered by the NSE's trading system, it became the leading stock exchange in the country in its very first year of operation. This forced the other stock exchanges to adopt SBTS. As a result, open out-cry system has disappeared from India. Today, India can boast that almost 100 per cent trading takes place through electronic order matching.

Technology has been harnessed to carry the trading platform to the premises of brokers. NSE carried the trading platform further to the PCs in the residence of investors through the internet. This has made a huge difference in terms of equal access to investors in a geographically vast country like India.

(d) Trading Cycle

Initially, the trading cycle varied from 14 days for specified securities to 30 days for others and settlement took another fortnight. The exchanges, however, continued to have different weekly trading cycles, which enabled shifting of positions from one exchange to another. Rolling settlement on T+5 basis was introduced in respect of specified scrips reducing the trading cycle to one day. It was made mandatory for all exchanges to follow a uniform weekly trading cycle in respect of scrips not under rolling settlement. All scrips moved to rolling settlement from December 2001. The settlement period has been reduced progressively from T+5 to T+3 days. Currently T+2 day settlement cycle is being followed.

(e) Derivatives Trading

To assist market participants to manage risks better through hedging, speculation and arbitrage, SCRA was amended in 1995 to lift the ban on options in securities. However, trading in derivatives took-off much later after the suitable legal and regulatory framework was out in place. The market presently offers index futures and index options on Nifty 50, CNX IT, Bank Nifty, Nifty Junior, CNX 100, Nifty Midcap 50, BSE 30 Sensex, BSE Teck, BSE Bankex, BSE

Oil and Gas, BSE PSU, BSE Metal and BSE FMCG. The mini derivative (futures and options) contracts on Nifty 50 and Sensex were introduced for trading in 2008.

(f) Demutualisation

Historically, brokers owned, controlled and managed the stock exchanges. In case of disputes, integrity of the exchange suffered. Therefore, regulators focused on reducing the dominance of trading members in the management of stock exchanges and advised them to reconstitute their governing councils to provide for at least 50% non-broker representation. The Securities and Exchange Board of India (SEBI), has approved and notified the Corporatisation and Demutualisation Scheme of 19 Stock Exchanges. This is a major step for modernisation of securities markets. India is the only country, which achieved this corporatisation and demutualisation in the shortest possible time. NSE and OTCEI, was the first exchanges in India to adopt a pure demutualised governance structure where ownership, management and trading are with three different sets of people. This completely eliminates any conflict of interest and helped NSE to aggressively pursue policies.

(g) Depositories Act

The earlier settlement system gave rise to settlement risk. This was due to the time taken for settlement and due to the physical movement of paper. Further, the transfer of shares in favour of the purchaser by the company also consumed considerable amount of time. To obviate these problems, the Depositories Act, 1996 was passed to provide for the establishment of depositories in securities with the objective of ensuring free transferability of securities with speed and accuracy. This act brought in changes by (a) making securities of public limited companies freely transferable subject to certain exceptions; (b) dematerialising of securities in the depository mode. In order to promote dematerialisation, the regulator has been promoting settlement in demat form in a phased manner in an ever-increasing number of securities. The stamp duty on transfer of demat securities has been waived. There are two depositories in India, viz. NSDL and CDSL. They have been set-up to provide instantaneous electronic transfer of securities.

To prevent physical certificates from sneaking into circulation, it has been mandatory for all new securities issued should be compulsorily traded in dematerialised form. The admission to a depository for dematerialisation of securities has been made a prerequisite for making a public or rights issue or an offer for sale.

(h) Risk Management

With a view to avoid any kind of market failures, the regulator/exchanges have developed a comprehensive risk management system. This system is constantly monitored and upgraded. It encompasses capital adequacy of members, adequate margin requirements, limits on exposure and turnover, indemnity insurance, on-line position monitoring and automatic disablement, etc. They also administer an efficient market surveillance system to detect and prevent price manipulations. The clearing corporation has also put in place a system which tracks online real time client level portfolio-based upfront margining. Exchanges have set-up trade/settlement guarantee funds for meeting shortages arising out of non-fulfilment/partial fulfilment of funds obligations by the members in a settlement. As a part of the risk management system, index-based market-wide circuit breakers have also been put in place.

The anonymous electronic order book ushered in by the NSE did not permit members to assess credit risk of the counter-party necessitated some innovation in this area. To address this concern, NSE had set-up the first clearing corporation, viz. National Securities Clearing Corporation Ltd. (NSCCL), which commenced its operations in April 1996. The NSCCL assured the counter-party risk of each member and guaranteed financial settlement.

NSCCL established a Settlement Guarantee Fund (SGF). The SGF provides a cushion for any residual risk and operates like a self-insurance mechanism wherein members contribute to the Fund. In event of failure of a trading member to meet his obligations, the fund is utilized to the extent required for successful completion of the settlement. This has eliminated counter-party risk of trading on the Exchange.

(i) Investor Protection

The SEBI Act established SEBI with the primary objective of protecting the interests of investors in securities and empowers it to achieve this objective.

SEBI specifies that critical data should be disclosed in the specified formats regarding all the concerned market participants. The Central Government has established a fund called Investor Education and Protection Fund (IEPF) in October 2001 for the promotion of awareness amongst investors and protection of the interest of investors.

Department of Economic Affairs and Department of Company Affairs, under Ministry of Finance alongwith SEBI and the stock exchanges have set-up investor grievance cells for redressal of investor grievance. The exchanges maintain investor protection funds to take care of investor claims. The DCA has also set-up an investor education and protection fund for the promotion of investors' awareness and protection of interest of investors.

All these agencies and investor associations are organising investor education and awareness programmes. In January 2003, SEBI launched a nation-wide securities market awareness campaign that aims at educating investors about the risks associated with the market as well as the rights and obligations of investors. The NSE have also taken special measures for educating the investors, it conducts seminars, workshops and comes out with advertisement both in print and electronic media to communicate to the investors.

(j) Globalisation

Indian securities market is getting increasingly integrated with the rest of the world. Indian companies have been permitted to raise resources from abroad through issue of ADRs, GDRs, FCCBs and ECBs. Further, foreign companies are allowed to tap the domestic stock markets.

Indian companies are permitted to list their securities on foreign stock exchanges by sponsoring ADR/GDR issues against block shareholding. NRIs and OCBs are allowed to invest in Indian companies. FIIs have been permitted to invest in all types of securities, including government securities. They can invest in a company under portfolio investment route upto 24 per cent of the paid up capital of the company. This can be increased up to the sectoral cap/ statutory ceiling, as applicable. The Indian stock exchanges have been permitted to set-up trading terminals abroad. The trading platform of Indian exchanges is now accessed through the Internet from anywhere in the world.

RBI permitted two-way fungibility for ADRs/GDRs, which meant that the investors (foreign institutional or domestic) who holds ADRs/GDRs can cancel them with the depository and sell the underlying shares in the market. The company can then issue fresh ADRs to the extent of the shares cancelled. Previously, once a company issued ADR/ GDR and if the holder wanted to obtain the underlying equity shares of the Indian company, then, such ADR/GDR would be converted into shares of the Indian Company. Once such conversion took place, it was not possible to reconvert the equity shares into ADR/GDR.

(k) Testing and Certification

With a view to improve the quality of intermediation, a system of testing and certification has been used in some of the developed and developing markets. This ensures that a person dealing with financial products has a minimum knowledge about them, the markets and regulations. As a result, not only the intermediaries benefit due to the improvement in the quality of their services, but also the career prospectus of the certified professionals is better. Thus, the confidence of the investors in the market increases.

NSE has evolved a testing and certification mechanism known as the National Stock Exchange's Certification in Financial Markets (NCFM). It is an on-line fully automated nation-wide testing and certification system where the entire process from generation of question paper, testing, assessing, scores reporting and certifying is fully automated. It tests practical knowledge and skills, that are required to operate in financial markets. A certificate is awarded to those personnel who qualify the tests, which indicates that they have a proper understanding of the market and skills to service different constituents of the market. It offers 14 securities market-related modules.

1.2 INTRODUCTION TO WORLD STOCK EXCHANGES

1.2.1 Introduction

A stock exchange, share market or bourse is a corporation or mutual organization which provides "trading" facilities for stock brokers and traders, to trade stocks and other securities. Stock exchanges also provide facilities for the issue and redemption of securities as well as other financial instruments and capital events including the payment of income and dividends. The securities traded on a stock exchange include: shares issued by companies, unit trusts and other pooled investment products and bonds. To be able to trade a security on a certain stock exchange, it has to be listed there. Usually there is a central location at least for record-keeping, but trade is less and less linked to such a physical place, as modern markets are electronic networks, which gives them advantages of speed and cost of transactions. Trade on an exchange is by members only. The initial offering of stocks and bonds to investors is by definition done in the primary market and subsequent trading is done in the secondary market. A stock exchange is often the most important component of a stock market. Supply and demand in stock markets is driven by various factors which, as in all free markets, affect the price of stocks.

There is usually no compulsion to issue stock via the stock exchange itself, nor must stock be subsequently traded on the exchange. Such trading is said to be off exchange or over-the-counter. This is the usual way that bonds are traded. Increasingly, stock exchanges are part of a global market for securities.

1.2.2 History

In 11th century France the courtiers de change were concerned with managing and regulating the debts of agricultural communities on behalf of the banks. As these men also traded in debts, they could be called the first brokers.

Some stories suggest that the origins of the term "bourse" come from the Latin bursa meaning a bag because, in 13th century Bruges, the sign of a purse (or perhaps three purses), hung on the front of the house where merchants met.

Stock Exchanges as a centre for trading were established only in the 16th century. In Antwerp, Belgium, traders gathered together in 1531 to speculate in shares and commodities. This was the world's first Stock Exchange and it was born in a city that was known for shipping and trading. Hamburg, in Germany, also a trade powerhouse, followed in 1558. Amsterdam came next, in 1619. London and Paris also set-up Exchanges sometime near the end of the 17th century.

It is interesting to note that in each case these stock exchanges were set-up in the most powerful business and trade centers of the day. They arose as a result of the dual need for financing by businesses, and for returns by those providing the finance. Whatever be the reasons, this was an idea whose time had finally come.

Almost a hundred years later, in 1792, came the New York Stock Exchange (NYSE). The last would be a seminal event—the NYSE is today one of the most powerful exchanges in the world. It was started when refinancing of government debt into tradable bonds, together with a stock issue by the Bank of the United States, had fueled rapid speculation in securities. Consequently, around 20 brokers decided it was worth their while to actually form an Exchange.

1.2.3 The World's First Joint Stock Company

It was, in 1553, when Sir Richard Willoughby, an explorer in London wanted to finance a venture to find a passage to the East. His company had a wild and romantic name—The Mysterie and Compagnie of the Merchant Adventurers for the Discoveries of Regions, Dominions, Islands and Places Unknown.

Its shares were offered to a small set of merchants. The issue was subscribed fully. The investors made a killing, for Willoughby's ship returned from Moscow with riches galore.

The Muscovy Company—as it was then called—had created a historic first. Of course, Willoughby died in the attempt. The Muscovy Company wasn't the first to actually come out with an IPO.

But, it created a buzz in the markets, and other large enterprises with projects on hand and hungry for money tried to emulate its financing strategy. Over a period of time, as this route of financing grew popular, entrepreneurs latched on to this mode of easy money.

The Dutch later started joint stock companies, which let shareholders invest in business ventures and get a share of their profits or losses. In 1602, the Dutch East India Company issued the first shares on the Amsterdam Stock Exchange. It was the first joint stock company to issue stocks and bonds. In 1688, the trading of stocks began on a stock exchange in London.

This was how stock market as a concept was born. The term 'stock' comes from a French term "souche" which means a stub or stump of a tree trunk, and refers to the tally upon which debts and claims were notched.

1.2.4 Growth—Early Days

In the early days, and for a long time, stock markets were not much more than conference halls. Their impact, however potent, was actually limited in comparison to other business activity. Insurance was one big game and so was debt.

However, in the 19th century this was to change dramatically. The huge impetus to industrial capitalism in 1800s meant that stock markets became the most efficient means of raising capital for industries shipping, railroads that burnt money at an unheard of rate. The evolution of capitalism in that century has been too well recorded in many other places for us to give it more than a brief mention.

However, it created an equity phenomenon that was to spearhead an equities revolution in the 20th century and make stock markets one of the most actively watched and followed financial institutions of the world. Popular heroes in the form of powerful investors were created and this resulted in the global penetration of trading activity.

It was in this period that the London Stock Exchange became one of the most powerful Exchanges in the world, in keeping with the superpower status of England at the time. Technological developments kept apace. In 1867, the New York Stock Exchange introduced its first ticker, quoting stock prices.

A transatlantic telegraph cable was completed the previous year, allowing traders in New York and London to communicate. And improved technology boosted trade. In 1886, the NYSE had its first million-share day; 25 years earlier, the average daily volume had been only about 1,500 shares.

The history of the stock markets in the 20th century has been well documented. It has been a century in which the markets have been transformed beyond recognition. The changes have been far too many and narration of them in detail would require a huge time. So we deal with a few key milestones but one important observation to be made is that the development of company form of organization and the growth of stock exchanges as institutions have been parallel.

1.2.5 Twenties and Great Fall

After the First World War (1914-19), there was a period of great economic prosperity. In the 1920s, many of the Dow Jones Industrial Average (DJIA) stocks rose more than five-fold in value. This spurred on investors with little or no knowledge of equities to make a quick buck.. All this came to a spectacular end. The crash of 1929 in New York, brought misery to one and all. It is said that brokers and bankers jumping out of skyscrapers was a common sight. On October 24, 1929, (Black Thursday) the Dow lost 30 per cent in value, thus signaling the end of a decade (known as the Roaring Twenties) of market growth. Paper millionaires became destitute overnight.

The mayhem ended in mid-1932, with the Dow down a whopping 90 per cent in value from its peak in 1929. The drop in stocks was worth $30 billion, which was about 30 per cent of the GDP. Soon afterwards the linkages between the markets and the economy was amply demonstrated, when the US entered its longest and deepest economic slump. It would take the Dow 25 years to get back to the highs established in 1929. The Great Depression, as the post crash slump came to be known is still remembered and studied in the US as a time of great despair.

The years 1929-54 are also known more for the structural reforms on Wall Street than any major speculative activity. In 1934, for instance, the Securities and Exchange Commission (SEC) was established to police Wall Street behaviour and protect investors from fraud. Also, after 1929, there was an increasing interest in study and development of techniques of stock market investment. As a result equity and technical research were given an added impetus. In these years also, came about the setting up and development of Exchanges all the world over.

The first great bull period came in the US in the 1950s, from 1954 to 1969. The 50s in particular were years of great economic prosperity for Americans and this was reflected in one of the longest bull runs in history; from 1954 to 1969.

The next decade was not be so good. The 1970s, in fact, were some of the worst years in stock market history. This happened in the aftermath of the oil shocks of the early 1970s, and the currency devaluations that followed.

Then came the merger mania induced bull run of the 1980s, the period that was dominated by the junk-bond king, Mike Milken and Ivan Boesky. There was another period of panic, "Black Monday," October 19, 1987, when the Dow lost 23 per cent in value on a single day. However, within a year the market was scaling new heights.

The next wave came about in the late 1990s the period everyone now refers to as the dotcom revolution. Too much has been said and written about this phase and to mention it here would be an overkill.

The last decade has witnessed a period of globalization wherein the economies have become linked with the other major economies of the world specifically the US economy. The last two years have seen the stock markets tumbling to lows on account of the world economic and financial crisis led by sub-prime mortgage in US and bursting of some of the leading and major investment banks and financial institutions in the world.

Table 1.4 shows the market capitalization of the top world exchanges. In American region the New York Stock Exchange (NYSE) is the leading stock exchange. In 2003 the market capitalization is 11328953 million US $ which has increased by 38.14% to 15650833 million US $ by the year end of the year 2007. The next is Nasdaq Exchange with a market capitalization of 2844193 million US $ in the year 2003 which has increased by 41.11% to 4013650 million US $ by the end of the year 2007.

In Europe-Africa-Middle East Countries, EuroNext Exchange which is a consolidated Exchange is on the top with the market capitalization of 2076410 million US $ in the year 2003 which has shown a tremendous increase to 103.36% to 4222680 million US $ by the end of the year 2007.Next to the EuroNext exchange is the London Stock Exchange (LSE) with a market capitalization of 2460064 million US $ in the year 2003 which has shown an increase of 56.56% to 3851706 million US $ by the end of the year 2007.

In the Asian-Pacific countries, the Tokyo Stock Exchange (TYSE) is the leading exchange with the market capitalization of 2953098 million US $ in the year 2003 which has increased by 46.65% to 4330922 million US $ by the end of the year 2007. Shanghai Stock Exchange is at second position with a market capitalization of 360106 million US $ in the year 2003 which has shown a whopping increase of 925.90% to 3694348 million US $ by the end of the year 2007.

Table 1.5 depicts the number of listed companies in top 20 world exchanges. In the Americas region the TSX group is leading among the others stock exchanges with 3951 listed companies by the end of the year 2007, which were 3599 in the year 2003, showing an increase of 9.78 per cent. The second in terms of listed companies is the Nasdaq Exchange which has 3294 companies listed in the year 2003 but the number decreased by 6.83 per cent to 3069 by the end of the year 2007.

In Europe-Africa-Middle-East countries BME Spanish Exchange is leading with 3537 listed companies by the end of the year 2007, however, the exchange had no listed company by the end of the year 2003. London Stock Exchange (LSE) is the next after BME Spanish Exchange in terms of listed

TABLE 1.4

Market Capitalization of Top World Stock Exchanges (End December 2007)

Exchange	*Market Capitalisation (Million US $)*				
	2003	*2004*	*2005*	*2006*	*2007*
American Region					
American SE	92877	83019	201403	282801	257797
Bermuda SE	2901	1852	2125	2704	2731
Buenos Aires SE	34995	40594	47590	51240	57070
Colombia SE	14259	25223	50501	56204	101956
Lima SE	14125	17975	24140	40022	69386
Mexican SE	122533	171940	239128	348345	397725
Nasdaq SE	2844193	3532912	3603985	3865004	4013650
NYSE	11328953	12707578	13632303	15421168	15650833
Santiago SE	87508	116924	136493	174419	212910
Sao Paulo SE	226358	330347	474647	710247	1369711
TSX Group	888678	1177518	1482185	1700708	2186550
Europe-Africa-Middle-East					
Amman SE	NA	18383.4	37644	29729	41216
Athens Exchange	103764	121921	145121	208256	264961
BME Spanish Exchanges	726243	940673	959910	1322915	1799834
Borsa Italiana	614842	789563	798073	1026504	1072535
Budapest SE	18868	28300	32576	41934	46196
Cairo and Alexandria SE	NA	38533	79509	93496	139274
Cyprus SE	NA	4880	6583	16158	29474
Deutsche Borse	1079026	1194517	1221106	1637610	2105198
EuroNext	2076410	2441261	2706803	3712681	4222680
Irish SE	85071	114086	114086	163269	143905
Istanbul SE	68379	98299	161538	162399	286572
JSE South Africa	260748	442525	549310	711232	828185
Ljubljana SE	7134	9677	7899	15181	2874
London SE	2460064	2865243	3058182	3794310	3851706
Luxembourg SE	37333	50144	51248	79514	166078
Malta SE	1845	2842	4097	4504	5633
Mauritius SE	NA	2103	2330	4959	7919
OMX Copenhagen SE	118167	NA	NA	NA	NA
OMX helsinki SE	170283	NA	NA	NA	NA
OMX Stockholm SE	293017	NA	NA	NA	NA
OMX Nordic Exchange	NA	728769	802561	1122705	1242578

Oslo Bors	95920	141624	190952	279910	353353
Swiss Exchange	727103	826041	935448	1212308	1271048
Tehran SE	27544	42600	36440	36315	43885
Tel Aviv SE	68904	90158	122578	161732	235056
Warsaw SE	37405	71547	93602	151809	211620
Wiener Borse	56522	87776	126309	199121	236448
Asia-Pacific					
Australian SE	585431	776403	804015	1095857	1298315
BSE, The SE Mumbai	278663	386321	553074	818879	1819101
Bursa Malaysia	160970	181624	180518	235581	325290
Colombo SE	2711	3657	5720	7769	7553
Hong Kong Exchanges	714597	861463	1054999	1714953	2654416
Jakarta SE	54659	73251	81428	138886	211693
Korea Exchange	298248	389473	718011	834404	1122606
National Stock Exchange of India	252893	363276	515973	774116	1660097
New Zealand Exchange	33050	43731	40593	44817	47486
Osaka SE	NA	NA	NA	191969	212178
Philippine SE	23190	28602	39818	67852	102853
Shanghai SE	360106	314316	286190	917508	3694348
Shenzhen SE	152872	133405	115662	227947	784519
Singapore Exchange	148503	217618	257341	384286	539177
Taiwan SE Corp.	379060	441436	476018	594659	663716
Thailand SE	119017	115390	123885	140161	197129
Tokyo SE	2953098	3557674	4572901	4614069	4330922

Source: http://www.world-exchanges.org/file/Focus1108.pdf (assessed on 12th May, 2009)

companies with 2692 listed companies by the end of the year 2003 which has increased by 22.84 per cent to 3307 by the end of the year 2007.

In Asia Pacific, Bombay Stock Exchange (BSE) has the highest number of listed companies at 4887 by the end of the year 2007, the number was 4730 in the year 2004. Tokyo Stock Exchange is the next with 2206 number of listed companies by the end of the year 2003 which increased by 9.42 per cent to 2414 by the end of the year 2007.

The above table also shows that Bombay Stock Exchange of India which is one of the oldest Exchanges in Asia is the leading exchange in the world in terms of listed companies.

TABLE I.5

International Equity Markets (Number of Listed Companies)

Exchange	*Number of Listed Companies*				
	2003	*2004*	*2005*	*2006*	*2007*
Americas					
American SE	557	575	595	592	599
Bermuda SE	55	58	56	54	53
Buenos Aires SE	110	107	104	106	111
Colombia SE	108	106	98	94	90
Lima SE	227	224	224	221	226
Mexican Exchange	237	326	326	335	367
Nasdaq	3294	3229	3164	3133	3069
NYSE	2308	2293	2270	2280	2273
Santiago SE	240	240	246	246	241
Sao Paulo SE	391	388	381	350	404
TSX Group	3599	3604	3758	3842	3951
Europe-Africa-Middle-East					
Amman SE	NA	192	201	227	245
Athens Exchange	332	341	304	290	283
BME Spanish Exchanges	NA	NA-	NA	3378	3537
Borsa Italiana	279	278	282	311	307
Budapest SE	51	46	44	41	41
Cairo and Alexandria SEs	NA-	795	744	595	435
Cyprus SE	NA-	124	119	141	141
Deutsche Borse	866	819	764	760	866
Eurnoext	1392	1333	1259	1210	1155
Irish SE	66	65	66	70	73
Istanbul SE	285	297	304	316	319
JSE South Africa	411	389	373	389	411
Ljubljana SE	134	140	116	100	87
London SE	2692	2837	3091	3256	3307
Luxembourg SE	242	234	245	260	261
Malta SE	13	13	13	14	16
Mauritius SE	NA-	29	30	63	70
OMX Copenhagen SE	194	183	NA	NA-	NA-
OMX helsinki SE	145	137	NA	NA-	NA-
OMX Stockholm SE	282	276	NA	NA	NA
OMX Nordic Exchange	NA	NA	678	791	851
Oslo Bors	178	188	219	229	248

Swiss Exchange	419	409	400	348	341
Tehran SE	345	402	408	320	329
Tel Aviv SE	577	578	584	606	657
Warsaw SE	203	230	241	265	375
Wiener Borse	125	120	111	113	119
Asia-Pacific					
Australian SE	1471	1583	1714	1829	1998
BSE, The SE Mumbai	NA	4730	4763	4796	4887
Bursa Malaysia	902	959	1019	1025	986
Colombo SE	244	242	239	237	235
Hong Kong Exchanges	1037	1096	1135	1173	1241
Indonesia SE	333	331	336	344	383
Jasdaq	NA	NA	NA	971	979
Korea Exchange	684	683	1616	1689	1757
National Stock Exchange of India	911	957	1034	1156	1330
New Zealand Exchange	208	200	185	182	178
Osaka SE	1140	1090	445	467	477
Philippine SE	236	235	237	240	244
Shenzhen SE	780	837	833	842	860
Shenzhen SE	505	536	544	579	670
Singapore Exchange	560	633	686	708	762
Taiwan SE Corp.	674	702	696	693	703
Thailand SE	420	463	504	518	523
Tokyo SE	2206	2306	2351	2416	2414

Source: http://www.world-exchanges.org/file/Focus1108.pdf (assessed on 12th May, 2009)

1.2.6 Conclusion

The foregoing analysis is indicative of the fact that the future of regional stock exchanges in India is grim. All the regional exchanges have ended in dismal failure as they did not had a sustainable business model. In the present circumstances all of them are clinically dead and are not conducting any business. The idea behind introducing major reforms in the Indian capital markets is to bring then at par with international standards, which is the call of globalised regime.

In the process of the global transition, three distinct types of exchange business models may be seen emerging. Each has its market niche and interacts with other exchanges through various forms of cooperation and competition. These new entities are called the Global Exchange, the Regional Exchange, and-the Diversified Exchange. These structures will form an interlocking lattice, with each exchange filling a distinct economic space and thriving on its specialities. Exchanges that are able to identify themselves in this context and organize their strategic development accordingly will have strong chances for success as businesses. Those that cannot, may grow less significant in international capital markets as market users find lower costs and more liquidity in other trading sites, both domestic and abroad.

Thus, need of the hour is that stronger players should join hands with the smaller ones to reap the benefits of synergy, as they also cannot thrive in isolation alone.

Notes and References

1. Max Weber, 'Economy and Society, Vol. I, Part 2, pp. 107-09, 161-64; Theory of Social and Economic Organisation, pp. 246-50, General Economic History, New York, 1961, pp. 207-09. Free market economy is one of the most important components of capitalism. The other essential components of capitalism are:
   a. Unrestricted struggle between autonomous economic groups;
   b. Money economy;
   c. Formally free labour;
   d. Unrestricted market freedom;
   e. Expropriation of the workers from the means of production; and
   f. Individual ownership.
2. W.R. Scott, Joint Stock Companies 1720, Three Vols. 1912 cited by Tom Hadden, Company Law and Capitalism, Weidenfeld and Nicolson, London, 1980, p. 10.
3. J.A. Schumpeter, The Theory of Economic Development, 1934. Schumpeter mentioned that: The possessor of wealth even if it is the greatest combine must resort to credit, if he wishes to carry out a new combination which cannot like an established business be financed by returns from previous production. To provide this credit is clearly the function of that class of individuals, which we call capitalist.
4. Tom Hadden, *op. cit.*, p. 29.
5. P.F. Drucker, "The New Realities", Mandarin Paperbacks, London, 1987, pp. 153-54.
6. Government of India, Ministry of Finance, Securities Laws (Amendment) Ordinance, 2004.

7. The Stock Exchange Official Directory, Vol. II, Weekly replacement issue dated April 24, 1989, Bombay, p. 1.
8. For details, see, Bipan Chandra, The Long-term Dynamics of the Indian National Congress, (Presidential Address) 46th Session, Indian History Congress, Amritsar, 27-29 Dec., 1985, p. 3.
9. V.K.R.V. Rao, "India Since Independence—Retrospect and Prospect" Selected Readings course material for Management Development Programme on Industrial Policy, Planning and Development, Indian Institute of Public Administration, (13-18 February, 1989), New Delhi, p. 8.
10. P.D. Ojha, "Investors and the Capital Market", RBI Bulletin, Bombay, December 1987, p. 1139.
11. See: A. Ramaiya, The Companies Act, Wadhwa and Company, Nagpur, 1991, pp. 37-43.
12. This calculation is based on the information provided in Company News and Notes, New Delhi, November, 1990, p. 46, and March 1990, p. 11.
13. Max Weber listed the following occupational and other groups in the middle classes.

    (i) entrepreneurs, (ii) executives and managers, (iii) intelligentsia, (iv) men from liberal professions, (v) small businessmen, and (vi) skilled and semi-skilled workers.
14. Indian Investment Centre, "Liberalisation of policy in industrial licensing, foreign investment and investment by NRI's", New Delhi, August 1989.
15. Ministry of Finance, Department of Economic Affairs, Report of the High Powered Committee on Stock Exchange Reform, 1985, p. 6. (hereinafter referred to as Patel Committee).

    Mr. M.R. Mayya, Executive Director, Bombay Stock Exchange defines the role of Stock Exchange as the 'nexus between the savings and investment of the community'.

    See M.R. Mayya, 'Do Stock Exchanges have a Future', *Economic and Political Weekly*, Bombay, February 1978, p. M-19.
16. Report of the High Powered Study Group on Establishment of New Stock Exchange, June 1991, pp. 59-62 (hereinafter referred to as Pherwani Committee Report).

ANNEXURE I-A

List of Stock Exchanges in India

Sr. No.	Stock Exchanges	Year of Formation
1.	OTC Exchange of India	1990
2.	The Uttar Pradesh Stock Exchange Association Ltd.	1982
3.	Jaipur Stock Exchange Ltd.	1989
4.	Madras Stock Exchange Ltd.	1920
5.	Cochin Stock Exchange Ltd.	1980
6.	Bangalore Stock Exchange Ltd.	1963
7.	National Stock Exchange of India Ltd.	1992
8.	Gauhati Stock Exchange Ltd.	1984
9.	The Ludhiana Stock Exchange Ltd.	1983
10.	The Calcutta Stock Exchange Association Ltd.	1830
11.	Bhubaneswar Stock Exchange Ltd.	1989
12.	The Delhi Stock Exchange Ltd.	1947
13.	Vadodara Stock Exchange Ltd.	1990
14.	Ahmedabad Stock Exchange Ltd.	1894
15.	Madhya Pradesh Stock Exchange Ltd.	1958
16.	Pune Stock Exchange Ltd.	1982
17.	Bombay Stock Exchange Ltd.	1875
18.	Inter-connected Stock Exchange of India Ltd	1998
19.	Coimbatore Stock Exchange	1996
	DERECOGNISED STOCK EXCHANGE	
20.	Hyderabad Stock Exchange "The Hyderabad Stock Exchange Ltd. (HSE) failed to dilute atleast 51% of its equity share capital to public other than shareholders having trading rights on or before the stipulated date, i.e. August 28, 2007. Consequently, in terms of section 5(2) of the Securities Contracts (Regulation) Act, 1956, the recognition granted to HSE stands withdrawn with effect from August 29, 2007.	1944
21	Magadh Stock Exchange SEBI vide order dated September 3, 2007 refused to renew the recognition granted to Magadh Stock Exchange Ltd.	1986
22.	Saurashtra Kutch Stock Exchange (SKSE) SEBI vide order dated July 6, 2007 has withdrawn the recognition granted to Saurashtra Kutch Stock Exchange Limited.	1989
23.	Mangalore Stock Exchange As per Securities Appellete Tribunal order dated October 4, 2006, the Mangalore Stock Exchange is a de-recognized Stock Exchange under Section 4(4) of SCRA.	1984

2

PERFORMANCE EVALUATION OF RSEs

This chapter deals with the evaluation of the performance of the regional stock exchanges. The economic relevance and performance evaluation of the institution of stock exchange lies in its effectiveness in performing successfully two basic functions: (i) to facilitate resource raising from the community for financing especially the corporate sector public sector activities; and (ii) to provide an organized market place for the investors to freely buy and sell securities.

The functioning of the stock exchange has therefore, to be such, so as to create a climate conducive to an active primary market (new issues market) and to ensure fair and efficient trading of the listed securities in the stock exchange (secondary market) and to establish a harmonious relationship between the two.

In other words, the institution of stock exchange is expected to facilitate the channelisation of savings especially from the household sector to meet the investment requirements of the productive sectors of the economy primarily by ensuring a market place, that provides liquidity to capital market instruments through fair and transparent trading practices. The responsibility therefore to ensure the harmonious relationship between new issues market and secondary market or stock exchange rests with the functioning of stock exchanges.

The discussion in this chapter has been divided into three sections. Section I is devoted to the evaluation of stock exchanges in raising the capital in the primary market. It also studies the evolution and growth of stock exchanges in the country through secondary sources of data. Further, the evaluation of the performance of regional exchanges is carried out by using primary sources of information. Here, an attempt has been made to understand the contribution of the regional exchanges in meeting the expectations of the investors. In this process, the strengths, weaknesses, factors responsible for the fall of business of regional exchanges and reasons for the poor operating performance have also been analyzed. Section II deals with the role of the regional exchanges in managing the illiquid and thinly traded shares. The main conclusions are given in Section III.

The analysis is based both on primary and secondary data. The sources of secondary data include available and published information from stock exchanges, internet, newspapers, magazines, research journals and libraries. The primary data has been collected through questionnaires and expert opinion. The analysis has three dimensions. First, the discussion relating to the role of regional stock exchanges in raising capital for the industrial sector in the country has been carried out. The history, growth and decline of the RSEs based on secondary sources also forms part of this discussion. Second, the analysis is confined to the primary data collected through survey by canvassing questionnaires and opinions of the respondents which include professionals in this area, academicians and brokers. Finally, simple statistical techniques like per centages, weighted averages and ranking of weighted averages are used to carry out the tabular analysis. Factor analysis technique has been used to ascertain the factors and their contribution towards the growth and decline of regional stock exchanges.

2.1 RESOURCES RAISED BY RSEs

The ability of the stock exchanges in raising funds from the primary market for financing the long-term requirements for both private and public sector is a very important function performed by the stock exchanges. The existence of active stock exchanges provide support for healthy primary market. The performance of the stock exchanges in the country can be studied and analyzed through their resource mobilization ability.

Table 2.1 gives a brief account of the resources mobilized from the primary market.

TABLE 2.1

Resources Mobilised from the Primary Market

Year	*Category-wise*					
	Total		*Public*		*Rights*	
	No. of Issues	*Amount (Rs. Cr.)*	*No. of Issues*	*Amount (Rs. Cr.)*	*No. of Issues*	*Amount (Rs. Cr.)*
1993-94	1143	24372	773	15449	370	8923
1994-95	1692	27633	1342	21045	350	6588
1995-96	1725	20804	1426	14240	299	6564
1996-97	884	14284	753	11565	131	2719
1997-98	111	4570	62	2862	49	1708
1998-99	58	5587	32	5019	26	568
1999-00	93	7817	65	6257	28	1560
2000-01	151	6108	124	5378	27	729
2001-02	35	7543	20	6502	15	1041
2002-03	26	4070	14	3639	12	431
2003-04	57	23272	35	22265	22	1007
2004-05	60	28256	34	24640	26	3616
2005-06	139	27382	103	23294	36	4088
2006-07	124	33508	85	29797	39	3711
2007-08	124	87029	92	54511	32	32518

Source: SEBI Handbook of Statistics, 2008.

Table 2.1 clearly depicts that there has been a tremendous increase in the capital mobilized through the primary market. The total capital mobilized both as a part of public and rights issue was Rs. 24372 crore in the year 1993-94 which has grown to Rs. 87029 crore in the year 2007-08, showing an increase of 257 per cent or 2.5 times. Further, the increase in amount collected through the public issues has been from Rs. 15449 crore in the year 1993-94 to Rs. 54511 crore in the year 2007-08, showing an increase of 252.84 per cent or almost 2.5 times. However, the number of total issues registered a decline, from 1143 in the year 1993-94 to 124 issues only in the year 2007-08. The number of public issues have declined from 772 in the year 1993-94 to only 92 in the year 2007-08 while the number of rights issue have declined from 370 in the year 1993-94 to only 32 in the year 2007-08. However, the capital raised through both public and rights issue have increased tremendously even though the number of such issues have fallen. This shows that stock exchanges have thus performed tremendously in raising capital resources for the industry in both public as well as private sector.

2.2 GROWTH AND PRESENT POSITION OF THE RSEs

The trading of securities in India was started in early 1873. The only stock exchanges operating in the 19th century were those of Bombay set-up in 1875 and Ahmedabad set-up in 1894. These were organized as voluntary non-profit-making associations of brokers to regulate and protect their interests. Securities trading at that time was a state subject and Bombay Securities Contract (Control) Act of 1925 used to regulate trading in securities. Later on, however, it became a central subject under the constitution in 1950.

Some leading brokers in 1908 formed "The Calcutta Stock Exchange Association". In the beginning of the twentieth century, the industrial revolution was on the way in India with the Swadeshi Movement; and with the inauguration of the Tata Iron and Steel Company Limited in 1907, an important stage in industrial advancement under

Indian enterprise was reached. In 1920, the then demure city of Madras had the maiden thrill of a stock exchange functioning in its midst, under the name and style of "The Madras Stock Exchange" with 100 members. However, when boom faded, the number of members stood reduced from 100 to 3, by 1923, and so it went out of existence. In 1935, the stock market activity improved, especially in south India where there was a rapid increase in the number of textile mills and many plantation companies were floated. In 1937, a stock exchange was once again organized in Madras under the name of "Madras Stock Exchange Association (Pvt.) Limited". In 1957 the name of this stock exchange was changed to Madras Stock Exchange Limited. Lahore Stock Exchange was formed in 1934 but it had a brief life. It was merged with the Punjab Stock Exchange Limited, which was incorporated in 1936.

The Second World War broke out in 1939. It gave a sharp boom, which was followed by a slump. But, in 1943, the situation changed radically, when India was fully mobilized as a supply base. On account of the restrictive controls on cotton, bullion, seeds and other commodities, those dealing in these commodities, found the stock market as the only outlet for their activities. They were anxious to join the trade and their number was swelled by numerous others. Many Stock Exchanges, The Uttar Pradesh Stock Exchange Limited (1940), Nagpur Stock Exchange Limited (1940) and Hyderabad Stock Exchange Limited (1944) were floated. In Delhi two stock exchanges—Delhi Stock and Share Brokers' Association Limited and the Delhi Stocks and Shares Exchange Limited—were floated and later in June 1947, amalgamated into the Delhi Stock Exchange Association Limited.

There were 23 recognized stock exchanges in India in the year 2003. Out of these Bombay Stock Exchange and National Stock Exchange are the two major bigger stock exchanges and rest are the smaller regional stock exchanges. BSE is 132 years old, NSE is 14 years old and it brought the screen-based trading system in India. Soon after the formation of NSE, the trading volumes in regional exchanges recorded a sharp decline and presently no business is transacted in any of these regional stock exchanges due to various reasons. The number of recognized stock exchanges have declined to 19 by the year ending 2008.

A description of the turnover on the stock exchanges during the years 1995-96 and 1996-97, soon after the formation of NSE and start of screen-based trading, is shown in Table 2.2. The turnover for the purpose of comparison includes only the cash segment or cash market turnover in case of all the stock exchanges. Except for the NSE and BSE the other regional exchanges are not permitted to trade in WDM and F&O. Hence for suitable and adequate comparison only the cash segment turnover of exchanges has been compared.

NSE and BSE together contributed 64.82 per cent of the total turnover in the year 1996-97 as compared to 51.98 per cent during the year 1995-96. Further one can observe tremendous increase of business on the NSE which grew by 332% as compared to previous year during 1996-97. On the other hand, the per centage share of turnover in the case of each of the fifteen regional stock exchanges was less than 1 per cent during this period. It was less than 5 per cent in three regional exchanges, less than 10 per cent in one and less than 20 per cent on remaining two exchanges including the BSE. It will not be out of place to mention here that in the year 1996-97, the total single sided turnover on all the stock exchanges in India was Rs. 646,116 crore as compared to Rs. 227,368 crore in the year 1995-96, reflecting an increase of 184.17 per cent.

A break up of the turnover of the top five exchanges, ranked by turnover in 1996-97, for the years 1995-96 and 1996-97 is presented in Figure 1.

The figure exhibits that on the basis of per centage increase of the turnover over the previous year, during 1996-97, the top five stock exchanges ranked were NSE, Mumbai, Calcutta, Delhi and Ahmedabad.

A comparison of the turnover of the stock exchanges for the period 1996-97 and 1997-98 is depicted in Table 2.3. The table shows significant increase in turnover of NSE soon after its formation in 1994 and this increase in turnover was facilitated and supported by the screen-based trading system

TABLE 2.2

Distribution of Cash Segment Turnover on Stock Exchanges in India during 1995-96 and 1996-97

Stock Exchanges	*Turnover (Rs. Crore)*		*Per centage of Total Turnover*		*Change over previous year (Rs. Crore)*	*Change over previous year*
	1995-96	*1996-97*	*1995-96*	*1996-97*		
NSEI	68,141	294,504	29.97	45.58	226,363	332.20
Mumbai	50,064	124,284	22.02	19.24	74,220	148.25
Calcutta	62,128	105,664	27.32	16.35	43,536	70.07
Delhi	10,076	48,631	4.43	7.53	38,555	382.64
Ahmedabad	8,786	20,533	3.86	3.18	11,747	133.70
Uttar Pradesh	2,373	16,070	1.04	2.49	13,697	577.20
Pune	7,071	9,903	3.11	1.53	2,832	40.05
Ludhiana	4,849	5,274	2.13	0.82	425	8.76
Bangalore	890	4,398	0.39	0.68	3,508	394.16
Vadodara	1,259	4,268	0.55	0.66	3,009	239.00
Magadh	1,629	2,755	0.72	0.43	1,126	69.12
Coimbatore	2,503	2,398	1.10	0.37	-105	-4.19
Madras	1,594	2,315	0.70	0.36	721	45.23
Jaipur	1,047	1,519	0.46	0.24	472	45.08
Cochin	1,803	1,401	0.79	0.22	-402	-22.30
Gauhati	619	484	0.27	0.07	-135	-21.81
Hyderabad	1,285	480	0.57	0.07	-805	-62.65
Saurashtra/Kutch	564	398	0.25	0.06	-166	-29.43
Mangalore	39	373	0.02	0.06	334	856.41
Bhubaneshwar	226	231	0.10	0.04	5	2.21
OTCEI	218	221	0.10	0.03	3	1.38
Madhya Pradesh	204	12	0.09	0.00	-192	-94.12
Total	227,368	646,116	100.00	100.00	418,748	184.17

Source: SEBI Annual Report, 1996-97.

FIGURE I

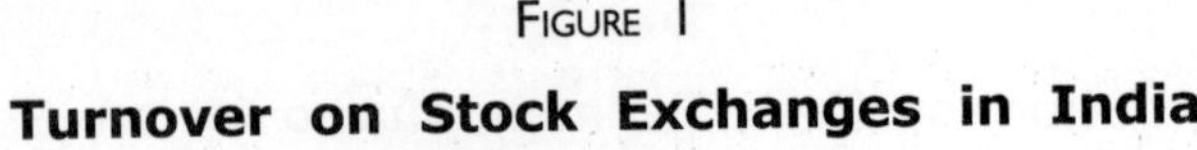

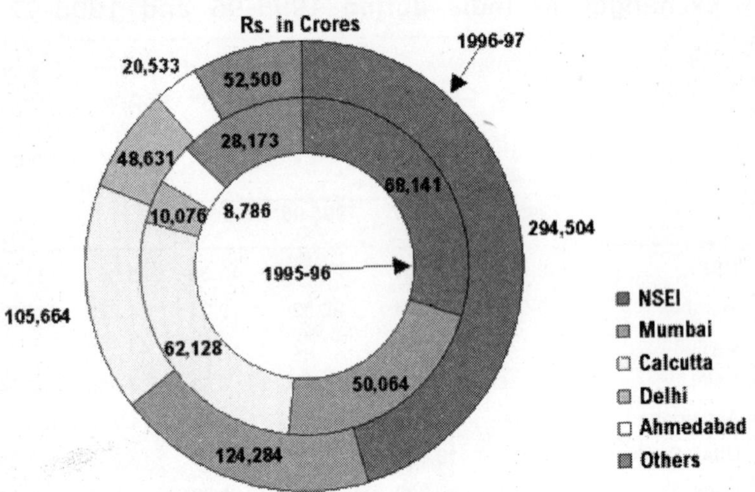

and expansion of BOLT facility across the country. In 1997-98, the total single sided turnover on the stock exchanges in India was Rs. 9,08,691 crore compared to Rs. 6,46,116 crore in 1996-97 and Rs 2,27,368 crore in 1995-96. The combined share of turnover of NSE and BSE shows a marginal decline, from 64.82 per cent in the year 1996-97 to 63.53 per cent in the year 1997-98. Further, in the year 1997-98 it can also be seen that the per centage of turnover to total turnover of stock exchanges was nil in the case of three regional exchanges, less than 1 per cent in thirteen regional exchanges, less than 10 per cent in three exchanges and less than 20 per cent in one exchange. The position of the regional stock exchanges thus further worsened.

The details of turnover of top stock exchanges are given in Figure 2. The aggregate share of the turnover of National Stock Exchange of India Ltd, Bombay Stock Exchange, Calcutta Stock Exchange, Delhi Stock Exchange and Ahmedabad Stock Exchange recorded an increase from 87.61 per cent in the year 1995-96 to 91.87 per cent in the year 1996-97 and further rose to 94 per cent in the year 1997-98. This reflects a fall in business of the rest of the regional stock exchanges.

TABLE 2.3

Distribution of Cash Segment Turnover on Stock Exchanges in India during 1996-97 and 1997-98

Sr. No.	Stock Exchanges	Turnover (Rs. Crore)		Pecentage of total all India Turnover	
		1996-97	*1997-98*	*1996-97*	*1997-98*
1.	NSEIL	2,94,504	3,69,934	45.58	40.71
2.	Mumbai	1,24,284	2,07,383	19.24	22.82
3.	Calcutta	1,05,664	1,78,778	16.35	19.67
4.	Delhi	48,631	67,840	7.53	7.47
5.	Ahmedabad	20,533	30,771	3.18	3.39
6.	Uttar Pradesh	16,070	15,390	2.49	1.69
7.	Pune	9,903	8,624	1.53	0.95
8.	Ludhiana	5,274	8,315	0.82	0.92
9.	Bangalore	4,398	8,636	0.68	0.95
10.	Vadodara	4,268	4,576	0.66	0.5
11.	Magadh	2,755	323	0.43	0.04
12.	Coimbatore	2,398	2,136	0.37	0.24
13.	Madras	2,315	1,228	0.36	0.14
14.	Jaipur	1,519	431	0.24	0.05
15.	Cochin	1,401	1,783	0.22	0.2
16.	Guahati	484	20	0.07	0.2
17.	Hyderabad	480	1,860	0.07	0
18.	SKSE	398	17	0.06	0
19.	Mangalore	373	308	0.06	0.03
20.	Bubaneshwar	231	202	0.04	0.02
21.	OTCEI	221	125	0.03	0.01
22.	MP	12	1	0	0
23.	Total	6,46,116	9,08,691	100	100

Source: SEBI Annual Report, 1996-97.

FIGURE 2

Per centage Share in the Total All India Turnover (in Rs.)

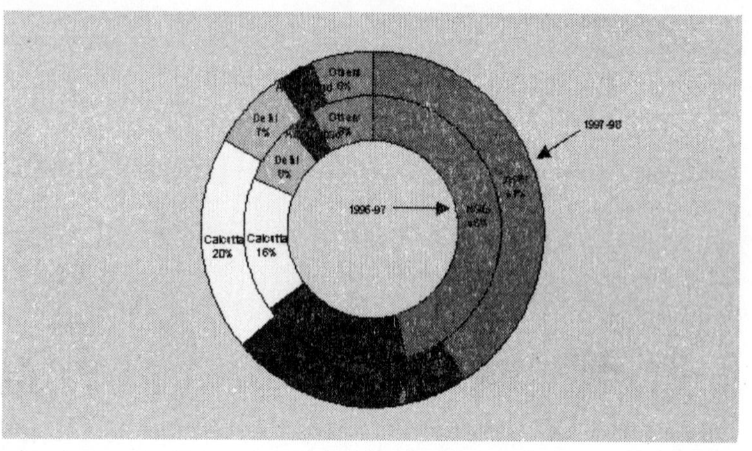

The values of the shares delivered in the equity segment of stock exchanges during the year 1997-98 is shown in Table 2.4. It can be observed that NSE and BSE together accounted for 94.46 per cent of the total delivery in rupee value terms. However, delivery at NSE and BSE compared to their own turnover was 15.97 per cent and 12.73 per cent in value terms. Thus, the trading activity was concentrated largely on the two exchanges namely NSE and BSE with the other regional exchanges lagging far behind in business.

This is also supported by the conclusions reached by another researcher Gupta Renu (2002).[1] who has observed that NSE reported higher turnover in the country than reported by most of the other regional stock exchanges. She has also reported that the combined market share of five major stock exchanges which include NSE, BSE, Calcutta, Delhi and Ahmedabad with respect to turnover of all stock exchanges show an increase from 87.6 per cent in the year 1995-96 to 97.2 per cent in the year 1999-2000.

In other words, 18 out of 23 stock exchanges (78.2 per cent) were doing business of 2.8 per cent of total turnover. The combined turnover of major five stock exchanges

TABLE 2.4

Delivery Patterns in Different Stock Exchanges During 1997-98

Name	*Turnover in Rs. Crore*	*Delivery in Rs. Crore*	*Delivery in Per cent*
NSEIL	369933.99	59091.18	15.97
Mumbai	207383.22	26399.79	12.73
Calcutta	178778.82	1954.58	1.09
Delhi	67840	760	1.12
Ahmedabad	30771	277.33	0.9
Uttar Pradesh	15390.14	201.8	1.31
Pune	8624.27	142.04	1.65
Ludhiana	8315.6	78.57	0.94
Bangalore	8636.98	143.75	1.66
Vadodara	4576.82	76.52	1.67
Magadh	323.76	0.64	0.2
Coimbatore	2136.89	12.24	0.57
Madras	1228.3	1185.19	96.49
Jaipur	431.39	10.68	2.48
Cochin	1783.86	49.35	2.76
Hyderabad	1860	75.16	4.04
Guahati	20.57	1.65	8.02
SKSE	17.51	1.19	6.8
Mangalore	308.81	8.72	2.82
Bubaneshwar	202.49	2.25	1.11
OTCEI	125.44	29.05	23.16
MP	1.31	0.05	3.82
Total	908691.17	90501.7	9.96

Source: SEBI Annual Report, 1997-98.

increased by nine times between the period 1995-96 to 1999-2000 as compared to an increase of 1.9 times of turnover of rest of the stock exchanges. Her study has concluded that the increasing trend of concentration of trading in major stock exchanges indicates that regional stock exchanges are loosing their business. Increasing monopoly of NSE requires restructuring of Indian stock exchanges with a view to providing justification for existence of regional stock exchanges.

The situation further deteriorated in the year 2001, after the abolition of badla system (Table 2.5A). The total turnover of business at 23 stock exchanges in the year 2001-02 declined significantly to Rs. 8,95,725 crore from Rs. 28,80,803 crore as compared to the previous year 2000-01. The performance of various stock exchanges can be viewed in terms of their share in total turnover of all the stock exchanges. The share of NSE in total turnover increased to 57.3 per cent in the year 2001-02 as compared to 46.5 per cent in the year 2000-01, while the share of BSE marginally decreased to 34.3 per cent in 2001-02. On the other hand, share of Calcutta Stock Exchange declined substantially to 3.0 per cent from 12.3 per cent and that of Delhi from 2.9 per cent to 0.7 per cent during the same period. It can be observed that several other regional stock exchanges like Bhubaneshwar, Jaipur, Guahati, Bangalore, Magadh, SKSE, Coimbatore reported nil or negligible turnover activity in the year 2001-02. The viability of these exchanges was further eroded.

Table 2.5A shows that after the year 2001-02, NSE and BSE accounted for 91.61 per cent of the total business transacted at all the exchanges in the country. While Calcutta, Ahmedabad and Uttar Pradesh Stock Exchanges accounted for rest of the turnover, all other regional exchanges did not transact any business and therefore reported nil turnover.

The current scenario presents even a more dismal picture (Table 2.5B). The two bigger national exchanges, NSE and BSE account for 99.98 per cent of the total business transacted at all the exchanges. All other regional stock exchanges have reported nil turnover during the period 2006-08.

TABLE 2.5A

Distribution of Cash Segment Turnover at Stock Exchanges in India in* 2001 and 2002

Sr. No.	*Stock Exchange*	*Turnove (Rs. Crore)* 2000-01	*Turnove (Rs. Crore)* 2001-02	*Percentage of Total Turnover* 2000-01	*Percentage of Total Turnover* 2001-02
1.	NSE	1339510.90	513166.92	46.49	57.29
2.	Mumbai (BSE)	1000031.55	307392.36	34.71	34.32
3.	Calcutta (CSE)	355035.35	27074.71	12.32	3.02
4.	Delhi (DSE)	83871.12	5828.00	2.91	0.65
5.	Ahmedabad (ASE)	54035.20	14843.54	1.88	1.65
6.	Uttar Pradesh	24746.73	25237.31	0.86	2.82
7.	Bangalore	6032.83	70.26	0.21	0.01
8.	Ludhiana	9732.24	856.61	0.34	0.1
9.	Pune	6170.53	1171.03	0.21	0.13
10.	OTCEI	125.90	3.73	0.00	0.00
11.	Hyderabad	977.83	41.26	0.03	0.00
12.	ICSE	233.05	55.35	0.01	0.01
13.	Madras	109.18	24.14	0.00	0.00
14.	Vadodara	0.91	10.12	0.00	0.00
15.	Bhubaneshwar	0.01	0.00	0.00	0.00
16.	Coimbatore	0.00	0.00	0.00	0.00
17.	MP	2.39	15.93	0.00	0.00
18.	Magadh	1.55	0.00	0.00	0.00
19.	Jaipur	0.00	0.00	0.00	0.00
20.	Mangalore	0.00	0.00	0.00	0.00
21.	Gauhati	0.04	0.03	0.00	0.00
22.	Cochin	373.22	26.60	0.01	0.00
23.	SKSE	0.00	0.00	0.00	0.00
	Total	2880990.53	895717.94	100.00	100.00

Source: SEBI Annual Report, 2002.

TABLE 2.5B

Distribution of Cash Segment Turnover at Stock Exchanges in India from 2006-08

(Rs.Crore)

Sr. No.	*Stock Exchanges*	*2005-06*	*2006-07*	*2007-08*	*Percentage of Total Turnover 2005-06*	*Percentage of Total Turnover 2006-07*	*Percentage of Total Turnover 2007-08*
1.	NSE	1569558	1945287	3551038	65.66	67.00	69.21
2.	BSE	816074	956185	1578857	34.14	32.94	30.77
3.	Calcutta	2800	694	446	0.11	0.02	0.00
4.	Delhi	0	0	0	0.00	0.00	0.00
5.	Ahmedabad	0	0	0	0.00	0.00	0.00
6.	Uttar Pradesh	1486	799	475	0.06	0.03	0.00
7.	Ludhiana	0	0	0	0.00	0.00	0.00
8.	Pune	0	0	0	0.00	0.00	0.00
9.	Bangalore	0	0	0	0.00	0.00	0.00
10.	Hyderabad	89	92	0	0.00	0.00	0.00
11.	ICSE/ISE	0	0	0	0.00	0.00	0.00
12.	Cochin	0	0	0	0.00	0.00	0.00
13.	OTCEI	0	0	0	0.00	0.00	0.00
14.	Madras	5	1.2	0	0.00	0.00	0.00
15.	Madhya Pradesh	0	0	0	0.00	0.00	0.00
16.	Magadh	91	0	0	0.00	0.00	0.00
17.	Vadodara	0	0	0	0.00	0.00	0.00
18.	Gauhati	0	0	0	0.00	0.00	0.00
19.	Bhubaneshwar	0	0	0	0.00	0.00	0.00
20.	Coimbatore	0	0	0	0.00	0.00	0.00
21.	Jaipur	0	0	0	0.00	0.00	0.00
22.	SKSE	0	0	0	0.00	0.00	0.00
23.	Mangalore	0	0	0	0.00	0.00	0.00
	Total	2390103	2903058	5130816	100	100	100

Source: www.sebi.gov.in

FIGURE 3

Per centage Share of Leading Stock Exchnages

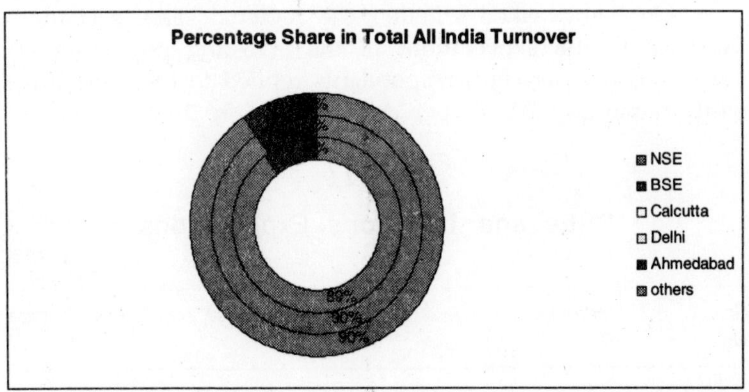

A cursory glance at Figure 3 reveals that during the period 2006-08 the entire business of securities trading in India was transacted on only two exchanges, namely, NSE and BSE.

2.2.1 Contribution and Strengths of Regional Stock Exchanges

That the RSEs became non-functional on account of various technological, administrative and institutional developments was clearly brought out in the foregoing analysis. In the following discussion, a modest attempt has been made to examine the various aspects of RSEs in order to arrive at logical conclusions which may point towards the revival of regional exchanges. A detailed survey conducted by us reveals some startling facts pertaining to the process of revival. The main results of the survey are discussed in the following paras. It is set in the order of understanding the (a) investors' expectations from regional exchanges, (b) analyzing strengths of RSEs, (c) analyzing weaknesses of regional exchanges, (d) knowing the reasons responsible for decline in the business of these exchanges, and (e) causes of their poor operating health.

(a) Investors' expectations from RSEs

Survey results pertaining to investors' expectations from regional exchanges are given in Table 2.6.

On being asked whether the regional stock exchanges lived up to the expectations of the investing population 85 out of 105 (81 per cent) respondents replied in the affirmative while remaining 20 (19 per cent) replied in the negative.

TABLE 2.6

RSEs and Investor's Expectations

(N=105)

Sr. No.	*Particular*	*Response*	*Per centage*
1.	Have met expectations	Yes	81
2.	Have not met expectations	No	19
	Total	100	

The survey results indicate that the eighty-five respondents (81 per cent) who had replied in the affirmative, felt that the regional stock exchanges had lived up to their expectations and these respondents identified the following strength factors of their stock exchanges (Table 2.7)

TABLE 2.7

Strength Factors of RSEs

(N=85)

Sr. No.	*Response*	*Per centage*
(i)	Easy reach to investors and brokers, etc.	100.0
(ii)	Financial Strength	60.0
(iii)	Physical Infrastructure	51.7
(iv)	Managerial Expertise	38.0
(v)	Meeting aspirations of small regional Investor	37.0
(vi)	Regional capital formation	27.05

(b) Strengths of Stock Exchanges

(i) Easy reach to investors and brokers

Easy accessibility or reach to the stock exchange facilitates the trading and primary market activities of the investor and the speculator. The brokers and the other intermediaries are located very well within reach of the stock exchange and many times within the stock exchange premises.

The response to the survey shows that all the respondents (100 per cent) replied unanimously that they have an easy physical access to the regional exchange to pursue their investment objectives due to nearness and approach to the broking facilities.

(ii) Financial Strength

Financial strength of any enterprise is important factor for taking decisions related to infrastructure upgradation including both process and technology upgradation.

The survey results show that in order of importance sixty per cent of the respondents replied that the exchange is providing services to the investing population due to its financial strength, which has helped the exchange to develop and add new and latest infrastructure as per the need of the hour. The financial strength of these exchanges have led to purchase of new and more spacious land with modern building architecture, providing individual offices and rooms to all the brokers, administrative staff and officers of the exchange. In some cases the excess infrastructure space created has been leased on rentals to banks and insurance companies. All the new infrastructure which has been created, is on modern lines with all amenities and facilities for the investors and visitors to the exchanges. Separate library facility, common room for investors with live trading screens at all open areas, in-house depository facilities and so on have also been included as a part of the infrastructure.

(iii) Physical Infrastructure

Infrastructure is one of the most important elements in growth of any enterprise today. The location as well as adequateness of infrastructure is very important for the growth of any enterprise.

The survey shows that over half of the respondents (51.7 per cent) were of the opinion that the regional stock exchanges had adequate infrastructure to support both ongoing and future activities. The new and the latest infrastructure which has been created, meets the growing demand of the investors and has been created on modern lines with all basic and modern amenities for facilitating all those who may visit the exchange. The buildings are spacious and take care of all the brokers who constitute the trading activities in the exchanges. Individual office space has been provided to all the brokers.

(iv) Managerial Expertise

Managerial expertise or quality of human resources along with adequate skills and technology know-how today is an important strength in any enterprise. The success and failure largely depend upon the approach of the management of the enterprise.

The survey reveals that about thirty eight per cent of the respondents opined that the managerial expertise in these exchanges was up-to-the-mark but further remarked that this was an area that requires improvement. Managerial expertise is yet another important strength for any enterprise to survive and sustain in long-term. The respondents further felt that more adequate professionals with finance, legal and investment background were required to manage these exchanges as they are in a better position to visualize change and act accordingly.

(v) Meeting aspirations of small regional investor

The regional exchanges have played an important role for meeting the aspirations of small regional investors who were provided with an opportunity to invest in regional companies which were known to him or mostly the management, industry or product mix was known, as being a local company. This information provided the investor with a reasonable confidence to invest in such companies and earn suitable return on his investment.

The survey shows that thirty seven per cent of the respondents felt that the regional stock exchanges were meeting the aspirations of the regional investors. They felt more confident in investing in regional companies as they had or could trace the history of promoters, quality of management or the nature of industry. This information made them take suitable decisions related to investment in these companies. The respondents further opined that the regional investor was provided with handsome opportunity to gain through these investment avenues and was happy to invest through regional exchanges.

(vi) Regional capital formation

The presence of regional exchanges also provided an opportunity to the regional entrepreneurs to raise capital in the market and get the company listed on the regional exchange where the regional investor could invest. The nearness or proximity of the exchange furthered his cause as he could receive all guidance and support from the regional exchange. The exchange in return was benefited by way of earnings in the from of listing fees.

The survey shows that twenty-seven per cent of the respondents felt that the regional capital formation has received a setback with less companies now coming out with public issues and moreover the regional companies which were being traded on these regional exchanges got themselves delisted which further aggravated the situation in the way that the regional exchanges lost their business and earnings by way of listing fees. The regional investor was badly hurt in the form of increase in non-traded or thinly traded shares as a result of delisting which meant that he could, no more sell or buy these shares and thus lost heavily the capital invested in such scrip's or companies.

The respondents, however, were of the view that the regional stock exchanges were providing meaningful service to the investing population despite no financial support from the government. The respondents were of the opinion that regional exchanges had played a significant role in development of conducive environment for facilitating growth in regional investment by providing platform to the investors to invest in regional companies and thereby also inducing the entrepreneurs in the region to conceive and plan big projects by throwing open the doors of investment through subscription in IPOs.

(c) Weaknesses of Regional Stock Exchanges

The survey further reveals that out of the twenty respondents who replied in the negative when asked whether the regional stock exchanges have lived upto their expectations, listed the following weaknesses of the regional exchanges (Table 2.8)

TABLE 2.8

Weaknesses of RSEs

(N=20)

Sr. No.	*Response*	*Per centage*
(i)	Limited number of companies for trading	85
(ii)	Non-transparent and inefficient trading and clearing mechanism	45
(iii)	Poor quality of governance board	35
(iv)	Inappropriate Technology	35
(v)	Non-resolution of Investor Grievances	20

(i) Limited number of companies for trading

Liquidity plays an important role for the investor and speculator in particular to trade in any stock exchange. The regional exchanges had few companies listed or the number of companies listed was few and further only a small number of these companies were traded on regular or daily basis. Regional exchanges providing small or less liquidity dampens the mood of the investor and he feels shy or stays away from trading in that scrip or share.

The survey reveals that eighty-five per cent of the respondents replied that the regional stock exchange lacked liquidity. By liquidity the respondents meant that they had limited choice to trade in a large number of listed and permitted securities. This is one prime reason for the investors to be alienated from the regional stock exchanges and move their business towards the national exchanges.

(ii) Non-transparent and inefficient trading mechanism

The trading mechanism should be transparent and followed by effective clearing and settlement of trades which is very critical for any exchange to survive. The investors confidence would certainly be eroded if the exchange defaults in settling the dues, timely.

The survey reveals that forty-five per cent of the respondents opined that the regional stock exchanges had not provided an efficient and transparent trading and clearing mechanism for the settlement of their trades until computerized trading and a uniform settlement was introduced by the market regulator. The brokers in RSEs were always looked with suspicion by the investor as to the rate of a particular deal being executed by the broker because the investor had no access to know the correctness of the price of the deal as he was not allowed any access to the trading hall of the stock exchange.

(iii) Poor quality of governance

Governance is perhaps one of the most important elements in growth of any enterprise today. The quality of the board and the top management is all important in guiding the growth and business sustainability of any organization. The governing board of the regional stock exchanges consisted of brokers who were the members of these exchanges also. The brokers were always interested in their own gains and many of them were illiterate to understand the intricacies of change or dynamics of change. They were busy with their own politics and gains at the cost of both the investor and the exchange. The role of independent directors and SEBI nominees was also limited as they either lacked expertise or knowledge about the trading or clearing mechanism and were further guided by the broker politics.

The survey shows that thirty-five per cent of the respondents were of the opinion that due to poor quality of governance or board, the regional exchanges were unable to sustain their business or growth. Further, the regional exchanges were always guided by the interest of the brokers or their political groups which guided the interest of the exchange to meet their own interest rather than the interest of all the stake-holders. This was also opined by the respondents as the main reason for demutualization or corporatisation of the regional exchanges so that their governance could become more professional as the independent directors on these demutulized exchanges would be experts from different financial areas and compliment their experience. This was necessary to bring in transparency in the functioning of these exchanges.

(iv) Inappropriate Technology

Technology appropriateness and adequacy is very important factor for deciding the business model of the exchange.

The survey reveals that thirty-five per cent of the respondents were of the opinion that the regional exchanges were facing lack of technology upgradation or possessed obsolete technology and were not fit for conducting trading operations. The respondents were of the opinion that regional exchanges had made no investment or had minimal investment in technology upgradation and followed the traditional outcry method or system of trading with a centralized trading ring. There was manual system of record-keeping, settlement process was slow and inefficient which led to delays in receiving payments by the investors who had sold their scrips or receiving shares by the investors who had bought the shares. This period was as long as 30 to 35 days. The screen-based online trading introduced by the NSE and BSE was an immediate success as it was well received by the investor community because it was transparent and accessible to remote areas. The settlement process was quickened and now the investor could receive his money in 3 to 4 days.

(v) Non-resolution of investor grievance

A healthy and sound investor grievance redress mechanism leads to building confidence amongst investors and gains the confidence in the functioning of the stock exchanges. It further brings transparency into the deals.

The survey shows that twenty per cent of the respondents were critical of the non-resolution of investor grievances and felt that the respective regional stock exchanges had inadequate grievance redress mechanism or were not functioning transparently, because of which the investors did not have confidence on the brokers or conduct of operations of the exchange.

(d) Decline in Business of RSEs

The primary survey further also listed and ranked the various reasons responsible for the regional stock exchanges being out of favour with the investing population which resulted in the fall of business. The respondents have ranked their opinion as per the Table 2.9.

TABLE 2.9

Factors Responsible for Fall of Business of RSEs

(N=105)

S. No.	*Factors of fall in business of RSE*	*Weighted Average*	*Rank*
(i)	Diminishing growth due to government policy and SEBI's role	15.33	1
(ii)	Growing problem of Illiquid/thinly traded stocks	13.96	2
(iii)	Preference of investors to trade on large exchanges	12.71	3
(iv)	Poor quality management of companies listed on the exchange	12.07	4
(v)	Loss of investor faith in RSE's	11.93	5
(vi)	Lack of economic and Industrial growth	10.82	6
(vii)	Shift of investor's Interest in Large Sized IPO's	10.00	7
(viii)	Lack of good corporate Governance by the exchange	9.60	8
(ix)	Less transparency in RSE's	8.87	9

(i) Diminishing growth due to government policy and SEBI's role

Government policies for providing adequate safety to investors and the subsequent role of regulator are important determinants for growth of business of RSEs. The steps taken by the regulator in this regard have hampered the conduct of business in the regional exchanges.

Government's Policy and role of SEBI with a weighted average mean score of 15.33 has been ranked at number 1 position as the most prominent factor responsible for fall of business of regional exchanges by the respondents. They are of the opinion that the government's policies related to functioning of the capital markets, and in particular, the secondary market or stock exchanges, were aimed at highest sense of investor protection. This shift in the government's attitude provided a larger role for the market regulator to achieve this objective. The regulator, thus, in the larger interest of the population moved to provide equal opportunity to the investors throughout the length and breadth of the nation by introducing real time access to trades through electronic trading, a transparent and uniform trading cycle across the country. The respondents opined that this policy found favour with the investors and they shifted their business interest from small regional exchanges to bigger exchanges like NSE and BSE. The brokers of regional exchanges thus lost their business to the bigger exchanges.

(ii) Growing problem of Illiquid/thinly traded stocks

The growing problem of illiquid or thinly traded stocks have made the regional exchanges no more the favourite trading exchanges. Though the regional companies were supposed to list themselves on the regional exchange, but doing away of this practice by the regulator resulted in many of these companies withdrawing themselves from regional exchanges to save the listing fee and further, most of these companies found themselves non-suitable for listing on larger exchanges like NSE and BSE as they did not meet their listing criteria.

Growing problem of illiquid or thinly traded stocks with a weighted average mean score of 13.96 has been ranked at number 2 position as another prominent reason for fall in business of RSEs. The respondents felt that the liquidity blocked in illiquid or non-traded/thinly traded scrips have had a negative impact on the business of the regional exchanges. Many investors find their money blocked in these scrips which were once traded on these regional exchanges but are no more traded after their closure.

(iii) Preference of investors to trade on large exchanges

The bigger stock exchanges, particularly the NSE has resulted in preference amongst the investors because of screen-based trading and uniform trading cycle.

Preference of investor's towards bigger exchanges like NSE and BSE with a weighted average mean score of 12.71 has been ranked at number 3 position as a factor responsible for fall of business by the respondents. The respondents were of the view that the rise of the national stock exchange resulted in problem of liquidity for the regional stock exchanges as more stocks were traded on the national exchanges and hence preference of the investing population to trade on the national exchange grew amongst the investors

(iv) Poor quality management of companies listed on the exchange

The quality of management of companies listed on the regional exchanges plays an important role in providing the investors with capital appreciation. The poor or weal managements seek to defy with the concept and thus would not like to provide the investor with appropriate capital appreciation or dividends. These are fly-by-night operators who collect money from the public and then forget about providing adequate returns to the investors.

Quality of management of companies listed on regional exchanges with a weighted average mean score of 12.07 has been ranked at number 4 position as another factor responsible for fall in business of regional exchanges. The respondents felt that it was the poor quality of management of the companies listed on these exchanges which has resulted in fall of business of these exchanges. These companies defied providing adequate safety of capital and returns to the investors and instead, the promoters have benefited in person and made huge profits by manipulating and price rigging of the share price thus resulting in loss to the common investor.

(v) Loss of investor faith in RSE's

The quality of management of regional exchanges along with transparency in buying and selling of shares at the regional exchanges lead to increased investor confidence in these exchanges. Any transaction leading to non-transparency and insider trading along with malpractices of the stock brokers are all to be dealt by the exchange authorities with determination and firmly so as to imbibe investor confidence in the trading mechanism of the regional exchanges.

Loss of investors' faith in the regional stock exchanges with a weighted average mean score of 11.93 has been ranked at number 5 position as a factor responsible for fall of their business. The respondents opined that the fall in business of regional stock exchanges is attributed to loss or lack of investor faith in functioning of these exchanges which were till now run by the broker community themselves with negligible or no role of independent professionals or directors. The regional stock exchanges according to them functioned by way of autocratic governance as their managing boards constituted largely the working brokers who were interested only in looking after their own interest. The trading mechanism and settlements were governed by the brokers' community without any role of independent professionals or authorities.

(vi) Lack of economic and industrial growth

The general economic conditions of growth and level of industrial activity in a particular region in the economy plays an important role in building conducive investment climate and leads to increased trading at regional exchanges.

General economic conditions prevailing in the economy with a weighted average mean score of 10.82 has been ranked at number 6 position by the respondents as yet another factor responsible for fall in business of regional exchanges. The respondents felt that it was the lack of economic and industrial growth in the region which has led to fall in business of regional exchange.

(vii) Shift of onvestor's interest in large sized IPO's

Primary market provides a good opportunity to those investors who would like to stay away or shy from active trading on the regional exchange.

Growing interest of investors in primary market with a weighted average mean score of 10 has been ranked at number 7 position as one of the factors responsible for fall in the trading business of regional exchanges. The respondents felt that the shift of the investors towards large sized IPOs has resulted in fall of business in secondary markets. The returns provided by these IPOs along with safety of capital was the reason responsible for this shift.

(viii) Lack of good corporate governance by the exchange

Lack of good corporate governance practices by the exchange leading to building of confidence amongst the investors also plays an important role in generating business at the exchange. The regional exchanges being managed by the brokers themselves who had majority ownership in management and administration provided a non-stimulus atmosphere for building right kind of investor confidence.

Lack of good governance practices in the regional exchanges with a weighted average mean score of 9.60 has been ranked at number 8 position by the respondents as another factor contributing towards fall in business of regional exchanges. The respondents felt that the business in the regional exchanges fell because of the lack of these good corporate governance practices. The brokers could not bring about professionalism in running of these exchanges and hence ruled over the much larger investor interest by overriding it with their own economic interest.

(ix) Less transparency in RSEs

Finally lack of transparency in functioning of the regional exchanges with a weighted average mean score of 8.87 has been ranked at number 9 position by the respondents as the last factor responsible for fall in their business. The respondents have contributed the fall of business at the regional exchanges to lack of transparency in operations that has eroded the confidence of the investing population in the regional exchange. They also opined that malpractices like insider trading, delay in settlement period and non-redressal of investor complaint or grievance and so on are some of the reasons where investors have lost faith in functioning of regional exchanges.

2.2.2 Poor Operating Health of RSEs

The survey reveals the factors which are responsible for the non-operativeness of the regional exchanges. These factors have been listed and ranked in Table 2.10.

Table 2.10

Factors Responsible for Non-operativeness of RSEs

(N=105)

S. No.	Factors Responsible for non-operativeness	Weighted Average	Rank
(i)	Poor governance	17.89	1
(ii)	Structural changes in financial markets	17.64	2
(iii)	Growing problem of non-traded/thinly traded shares	16.21	3
(iv)	Inter-exchange Competition	15.79	4
(v)	Decline in Listing fee	13.79	5
(vi)	Loss of investor faith in RSEs	12.00	6
(vii)	Inappropriate Technology	11.68	7

(i) Poor Governance

One of the prominent factor responsible for growth of any enterprise is the quality of the governance. The regional exchanges had majority of directors who were member brokers of the regional exchange also.

Poor composition of board or governance with a weighted average mean score of 17.89 has been ranked at number 1 position as the most prominent factor responsible for poor operating health of regional exchanges. While interacting with the respondents brokers it was opined that prior to demutualization of exchanges, the fellow brokers who were elected to the board of the regional exchanges were those who served the interest of the broker's group who got them elected. It was further pointed by the respondents that many of these brokers were neither having knowledge or foresight or expertise to lead the regional exchanges against dynamic changes happening in the capital markets. They were not prepared to take on the challenges posed by the NSE or BSE which were growing due to appropriate technology which helped them reach far-off places and brought transparency into the trading mechanism thereby reposing increased investor confidence.

(ii) Non-preparedness of regional exchanges towards structural changes

Structural changes in the financial markets along with more active role of regulatory authority and globalization of the business and financial markets led to newer role for regional stock exchanges which failed to visualize these dynamic changes. Formation of National Stock Exchange in 1994 and further the introduction of online trading by Bombay Stock Exchange which being the oldest and largest regional stock exchange in the country further deteriorated the conditions of the other regional exchanges as most of the business from small regional exchanges shifted to these two bigger exchanges.

Structural changes in the financial markets with a weighted average mean score of 17.64 has been ranked at number 2 position as another important factor responsible for the downfall of the regional exchanges. The respondents further listed these structural changes as globalization of financial markets, introduction of screen-based online trading by NSE and BSE, uniform trading cycle, demutualization of exchanges, introduction of derivatives trading and introduction of depositories. They further opined that the reach of NSE to almost all corners of the country with screen-based trading virtually halted the businesses at the regional exchanges which could not match the technology and were not prepared to take on these challenges.

(iii) Growing problem of non-traded/thinly traded shares

Regional exchanges had a number of local companies which were mandatory to be listed on these regional exchanges. Poor quality of management of these companies led to fewer trades and the number of companies which were actually traded on the regional exchange were too few. The final decision of SEBI to provide option to regional companies to delist from the regional exchanges was a final blow in this regard.

Problem of non-traded and thinly traded shares with a weighted average mean score of 16.21 has been ranked at number 3 position as another reason for non-operativeness of the regional exchanges. The respondents further felt that growth in number of non-traded and thinly traded regional companies scrips' moved the investors interest from regional exchanges to bigger exchanges, where large number of scrips were available to trade. The trading activity was a direct source of revenue for the regional exchanges in form of turnover fees which was levied on all transactions conducted by the brokers of these exchanges. The shifting of trading interest to bigger exchanges and problem of non-traded or thinly traded shares has led to considerable fall in revenue and the regional exchanges have almost no source of revenue from trading activities as trading diminished from these exchanges to the bigger exchanges.

(iv) Inter-exchange Competition

Inter-exchange competition amongst the various small regional exchanges and with bigger stock exchanges on the other hand is also an important factor for this study.

Lack of inter-exchange competition opportunities amongst the regional exchanges on one hand and their competition with bigger exchanges with a weighted average mean score of 15.79 has been ranked at number 4 position as another factor that has led to closure of the smaller regional stock exchanges. The bigger exchanges have led from the front and have taken over almost all business activities from these exchanges making them unviable.

(v) Declining Listing Fee

Listing fee is the most important component as a source of revenue for the stock exchanges. The companies whose shares are traded on these exchanges have to pay an annual listing fee to the exchanges which becomes their source of revenue.

Decline or fall in listing fee which was one of the most important source of revenue for the regional exchanges with a weighted average mean score of 13.79 has been ranked at number 5 position as another factor responsible for making them non-operative. The respondents were further of the view that the decision of the regulator to provide option of delisting to the regional companies, led to substantial decrease of income of these exchanges. With most of the companies already not been actively traded and the others getting themselves delisted, these developments completed ruined the operating health of the regional exchanges.

(vi) Loss of investor faith in RSEs

The faith of any investor in the stock exchange system and trading mechanism is important factor for the growth of the business of the exchange. The investors are inclined to invest or trade through the brokers registered with the recognized regional exchanges because they have faith and trust in the representatives of these exchanges which are controlled by the Ministry of Finance and SEBI as the regulatory body.

Growing loss of faith of the investors in the systems and trading mechanism along with delayed settlement procedures with a weighted average mean score of 12.00 has been ranked at number 6 position as another prominent factor leading to downfall of the regional exchanges. The respondents further opined that the brokers of these regional exchanges who enjoyed a majority on the board, had lost faith and trust of the investors due to non-transparent trading mechanism and delayed settlement procedures adopted by the regional exchanges. The dominance of superior technology which was provided by the two bigger exchanges was a shot in the arm in this regard as the outcry system was replaced by the screen-based trading where the investor could sit in front of the screen and see the different trades and rates of shares of different companies on the screen and make decisions accordingly. This led to complete adoption of technology by the investors who had already deteriorated their faith and trust in brokers of regional exchanges. The business from the regional exchanges thus moved to bigger exchanges.

(vii) Inappropriate Technology

Technology is another important factor for sustaining the growth or responsible for operating health of any enterprise. The regional exchanges could not update on technology front and thus lost the survival battle to bigger exchanges as the business model adopted by smaller regional exchanges failed to sustain against the superior technology of the bigger exchanges.

Inappropriate and poor technology available with the regional exchanges with a weighted average mean score of 11.68 has been ranked at number 7 position as yet another factor which led to poor operating health of the regional exchanges by the respondents. They further opined that the screen-based trading mechanism introduced by the bigger exchanges had far reach and coverage of the geographical area on one hand and also led to transparency in trading, thereby restoring or shifting investor interest from regional exchanges to bigger exchanges.

2.2.3 Factor Analysis

Factor analysis was conducted to study growth and decline of regional stock exchanges. The analysis reveals that growth depends upon a number of factors which were listed by the respondents participating in the opinion survey, these are total market size, number of listed companies and their quality of management, total number and growth in the number of investors in the region, total market float of the company, pattern of share ownership, growth in unit holders, level of investor education, regional contribution to absorb initial public offers, level of economic conditions prevailing in the region, entrepreneurial skills and drive in the region.

TABLE 2.11

Factor Analysis—Communalities(a)

	Initial	*Extraction*
Low regional market size	1.000	.510
Too few listings	1.000	.638
Limited free float and supply-demand imbalance of shares listed on the rse	1.000	.635
Stagnation in number of shareholders	1.000	.595
Inadequate growth of unit holders in mutual funds	1.000	.575
Statutory minimal share ownership	1.000	.780
Lack of market education and awareness	1.000	.749
Lack of broad investor base to absorb ipo's	1.000	.697

Extraction Method: Principal Component Analysis.

TABLE 2.12

Total Variance Explained

Component	*Initial Eigenvalues*		
	Total	*% of Variance*	*Cumulative %*
1	1.976	21.960	21.960
2	1.446	16.066	38.027
3	1.212	13.465	51.491
4	1.039	11.541	63.032

TABLE 2.13

Component Matrix(a)

	Component				
	1	*2*	*3*	*4*	*Extraction*
Low regional market size	.589	.301	.084	-.255	.510
Too few listings	.586	.437	.194	-.256	.638
Limited free float and supply-demand imbalance of shares listed on the rse	.217	.559	-.149	.504	.635
Stagnation in number of shareholders	-.281	.627	-.317	.148	.595
Inadequate growth of unit holders in mutual funds	.440	-.481	.165	.350	.575
Statutory minimal share ownership	-.087	.208	.601	.607	.780
Lack of market education and awareness	-.164	.119	.801	-.260	.749
Lack of broad investor base to absorb ipo's	.701	-.365	-.112	.244	.697

Extraction Method: Principal Component Analysis.

However out of the above listed factors only those are studied in the present study that are related to retarded growth or slow down in the growth of regional stock exchanges. The present study indicates that retarded growth is related to factors like Low regional market size, too few listings, limited free float, stagnation in number of shareholders, inadequate growth of unit holders, statutory minimal share ownership, lack of market education and lack of broad investor base to absorb initial public offers with factor loading of .589, .586, .559, .627, .440, .607, .801 and .701 respectively.

TABLE 2.14

Rotated Component Matrix(a)

	Component			
	1	2	3	4
Low regional market size	.712	.052	-.008	.018
Too few listings	.786	-.023	.122	.071
Limited free float and supply-demand imbalance of shares listed on the rse	.197	.008	.037	.771
Stagnation in number of shareholders	-.035	-.525	-.110	.554
Inadequate growth of unit holders in mutual funds	.002	.753	.077	-.040
Statutory minimal share ownership	-.146	.176	.751	.405
Lack of market education and awareness	.135	-.212	.749	-.353
Lack of broad investor base to absorb ipo's	.266	.757	-.226	.048

Extraction Method: Principal Component Analysis.
Rotation Method: Varimax with Kaiser Normalization: A Rotation converged in 13 iterations.

It is observed that maximum factor loading of .801 is given to lack of market education and minimum factor loading is in case of inadequate growth of unit holders. A large number of respondents feel that lack or inadequate market knowledge or education has been the main factor responsible for inadequate growth of RSEs. The investors operating in these regional stock exchanges have not had proper education upon the effect of globalization and integration of world capital markets and have thus lost considerable money and capital due to poor selection of stocks and have been unable to understand the market timings and trading strategies of FIIs *vis-a-vis* Indian Mutual Funds. These small investors have faced the burnt and have lost their considerable portion of investable surplus in the bouts of technical rally and subsequent corrections that followed. In absence of adequate market education these investors were unable to sell or buy equities in these RSEs at the correct time and thus incurred huge losses and lost faith in the RSEs.

At the same time these respondents also feel that inadequate growth of unit holders of mutual funds have least contributed towards the growth of RSEs among the various factors as selected above.

However, it is also revealed that factors like lack of broad investors (.701), stagnation in number of shareholders (.627) and statutory minimal share ownership (.607) are also some of the main factors which the respondents feel are important towards inadequate growth of RSEs.

This study reveals that the knowledge about the stock markets, especially in global scenario with the entry of large number of FIIs *vis-à-vis* Indian Mutual Funds has adversely impacted the fate of small investors attached to these RSEs. These small investors had little education about the market movements or swings caused by the FII activities in this changed scenario, where the markets were dominated by these big players.

2.3 ROLE OF RSEs IN MANAGING NON-LIQUID, THINLY TRADED OR NON-TRADED STOCKS

The growing problem of illiquidity of stocks is a big problem which needs an urgent solution in the larger interest of investors. Following a directive of the Securities and Exchange Board of India (SEBI), the Bombay Stock Exchange (BSE) and the National Stock Exchange (NSE), on the basis of the criteria agreed upon between the two bourses and SEBI, have classified 1,585 shares constituting 59 per cent of the traded stocks on BSE and 304 shares accounting for 22 per cent of the stocks traded on NSE as illiquid securities during the month of June 2008.

In 2007-08, of the 7,681 shares listed on the BSE, only 2,709 (35.3 per cent) were traded, while on the NSE, the securities of 1,244 companies, i.e. 90.1 per cent of 1,381 listed companies were traded. The rest were not traded even on a single day in the year. Both on the BSE and the NSE, 85-90 per cent of the traded shares were traded for more than 100 days in a total of 251 trading days.

These shares cannot strictly be called liquid. Liquid stocks are those which one can buy or sell at around the ruling market price. Except the top 100 shares, the impact cost in terms of spreads between bids and offers in respect of the remaining shares are quite wide, exceeding 2-3 per cent.

Even categorizing the securities traded for more than 100 days as liquid, the rest can be categorized as thinly or marginally traded securities, while all other securities not traded even for a day in a year are illiquid securities. Listed securities can thus be categorized under three heads—highly traded, thinly or marginally traded, and illiquid.

There are three major reasons for lack of liquidity. First, the equity base of the listed stocks of a large number of companies is quite low. There are several companies with equity capital of less than Rs. 3 crore due to historical reasons, such as low base of capital, public holding, etc. Second, the floating stock of listed securities, particularly those held by the public, is quite low. This is substantiated by the discussion paper issued by the Ministry of Finance in June 2007, wherein it is claimed that only about 42 per cent of the shares listed on the NSE constituted the floating stock, of which the public held a meager 13.35 per cent. The share of retail individual investors (RIIs) was hardly 5 to 6 per cent. Third, there are no market-makers or specialists, as in almost all the developed markets.

The survey conducted amongst the respondents as observed from Table 2.15 reveals that forty one per cent of the respondents were positive about the role of regional stock exchanges in the promotion of equity cult and the spread of the capital markets while the rest fifty-nine per cent of respondents opined that regional exchanges did not have much role in promoting the equity cult and spread of capital markets. The regional listing criteria was held to be main reason behind this. The mandatory regional listing on the regional exchange on one hand provided opportunities for the investors of the region to trade in that scrip but on the other

Table 2.15

Role of RSEs in Promoting Equity Cult

(N=105)

Particular	*Number*	*Per centage*
Positive role	43	41
Non-positive role	62	59

hand restricted the opportunities for trading at national level or other exchanges.

Further interaction with the respondents revealed that they were of the opinion that regional stock exchanges should provide for one time waiver of listing fee for all regional companies listed previously to provide for renewed trading in the stocks of these regional companies. The concept of market-maker or specialist must be introduced for thinly or marginally traded shares. Some of the respondents also opined that a call auction system should be introduced for thinly or marginally traded shares and the settlement period for such scrips should be enhanced to a week or fortnight. There should also be a provision of market-maker or specialist for new issues and the minimum public holding in such companies should be enhanced to 40 per cent of the issued capital.

Factor Analysis

Factor analysis was conducted to study the factors that contribute towards the economic operations of the regional exchanges. The respondents listed various factors like cost efficiency for all the stake-holders, inter-exchange competition, badla financing, volatility in market index, complexities in operations, level of capital expenditure, level of actual settlement, general level of liquidity and so on as factors which effect the functioning of stock exchanges.

Amongst the factors which directly contribute towards the economic operations of the RSEs, the respondents feel that division of liquidity and distortion of price discovery, cost inefficiency for all stakeholders, complexities in operations, lack of inter-exchange competition, limited revenue, inequitable burden sharing, low level of capital expenditure, no financial guarantee, low levels of actual settlement, concentration of liquidity, market capitalization, dominance of badla financing and excessive volatility are some of the important economic factors with factor loading of .751, .749, .757, .786, .649, .574, .559, .602, .559, .627, .753 and .607 respectively.

Factor analysis reveals that maximum factor loading of .786 is observed in lack of inter-exchange competition. The

TABLE 2.16

Factor Analysis—Communalities(b)

	Initial	*Extraction*
Ineffective regulation of members	1.000	.750
Ineffective regulation of listed companies	1.000	.647
Unequal access to corporate announcements	1.000	.578
Non-performance of outside directors (non-member directors)	1.000	.655
Division of liquidity and distortion of price discovery	1.000	.615
Cost inefficiency for all stakeholders	1.000	.636
Complexities in operations	1.000	.694
Lack of inter exchange competition	1.000	.710
Limited revenue	1.000	.661
Inequitable burden sharing	1.000	.633
Low level of capital expenditure	1.000	.620
No financial guarantee	1.000	.594
Few professionals	1.000	.545
Lack of training and development	1.000	.649
Inability to develop new products and services	1.000	.683
Low levels of actual settlement	1.000	.627
Concentration of liquidity and market capitalization	1.000	.657
Dominance of badla financing	1.000	.696
Excessive volatility	1.000	.703
Weak criteria to become a member	1.000	.564
Weak criteria to become a broker	1.000	.684
Weak criteria to become a market maker	1.000	.666
Barrier to entry of new intermediaries	1.000	.646
Membership card treated as investment instrument	1.000	.546
Low capitalization of brokers	1.000	.595
A single class of brokers	1.000	.511
Inadequate investor protection	1.000	.623

Extraction Method: Principal Component Analysis.

TABLE 2.17

Total Variance Explained

Component	*Initial Eigenvalues*		
	Total	*% of Variance*	*Cumulative %*
1	2.791	10.336	10.336
2	2.273	8.419	18.755
3	2.052	7.602	26.357
4	1.993	7.380	33.737
5	1.647	6.101	39.837
6	1.430	5.295	45.132
7	1.360	5.038	50.170
8	1.302	4.823	54.993
9	1.122	4.156	59.149
10	1.057	3.913	63.063

respondents feel that RSEs have not been able to provide enough opportunities for the investors as well the brokers to compete amongst each other, which according to them is a major factor contributing towards the poor economic health of these exchanges. The mandatory regional listings of the companies on the regional stock exchange under whose ambit the company felt also was cited as one of the reason for distorting the inter exchange trading. Each of these regional exchange mostly traded in shares of its own listed companies and could not compete well with national exchange like NSE. This was a major cause for increase in number of illiquid/ thinly traded or non-liquid shares, as regional listed companies provided constituted most of the trading opportunities for the regional investors. Further, once the regional stock exchanges were out of business, the regional companies had no platform to get their shares listed except for BSE or NSE but most of them were not able to meet the stringent listing criteria of these bigger exchanges and thus found no active trades. Amongst the RSEs only BSE could survive as it was perceived as a national exchange before the emergence of NSE and maximum numbers of regionally listed companies were also traded on BSE.

Least factor loading of .559 was observed in two factors, namely, low level of capital expenditure and low

TABLE 2.18

Component Matrix(b)

	Component				
	1	*2*	*3*	*4*	*Extraction*
Ineffective regulation of members	.649	.215	-.135	.349	.750
Ineffective regulation of listed companies	.197	.687	.037	.197	.647
Unequal access to corporate announcements	-.035	.525	.110	-.035	.578
Non-performance of outside directors (non-member directors)	.452	.753	.077	.002	.655
Division of liquidity and distortion of price discovery	-.146	.176	.751	-.146	.615
Cost inefficiency for all stakeholders	.135	-.212	.749	.135	.636
Complexities in operations	.266	.757	-.226	.266	.694
Lack of inter-exchange competition	.301	.112	.786	-.023	.710
Limited revenue	.437	.621	.649	.215	.661
Inequitable burden sharing	.191	.574	.197	.008	.633
Low level of capital expenditure	.559	-.357	.084	.543	.620
No financial guarantee	.602	.148	.194	.627	.594
Few professionals	.567	.350	-.047	-.481	.545
Lack of training and development	.579	.194	-.256	.208	.649
Inability to develop new products and services	.191	.634	-.124	.119	.683
Low levels of actual settlement	.559	-.149	.504	-.365	.627
Concentration of liquidity and market capitalization	.627	-.317	.148	.432	.657
Dominance of badla financing	-.481	.165	.350	.753	.696
Excessive volatility	.208	.601	.607	.589	.703
Weak criteria to become a member	.119	.801	-.260	.586	.564
Weak criteria to become a broker	.601	-.281	.231	.663	.684
Weak criteria to become a market maker	.801	.440	.342	.217	.666
Barrier to entry of new intermediaries	-.112	-.087	.543	.654	.646
Membership card treated as investment instrument	.751	.301	.112	.786	.546
Low capitalization of brokers	.749	.437	.621	.649	.595
A single class of brokers	-.226	.191	.574	.197	.511
Inadequate investor protection	.432	.602	.342	.264	.623

TABLE 2.19

Rotated Component Matrix(a)

	Component									
	1	*2*	*3*	*4*	*5*	*6*	*7*	*8*	*9*	*10*
1	*2*	*3*	*4*	*5*	*6*	*7*	*8*	*9*	*10*	*11*
Ineffective regulation of members	.212	-.102	-.414	.150	.069	-.268	-.362	.236	-.208	-.440
Ineffective regulation of listed companies	.512	-.310	-.055	.054	.009	-.251	-.081	.344	-.261	.165
Unequal access to corporate announcements	.245	-.010	.525	-.259	-.123	-.070	.138	-.343	-.116	.066
Non-performance of outside directors (non-member directors)	.560	-.272	.171	-.104	-.300	-.298	-.052	.011	.213	.012
Division of liquidity and distortion of price discovery	.321	-.325	.212	.240	.141	.242	.196	.180	-.379	-.102
Cost inefficiency for all stakeholders	.304	-.156	-.237	.085	-.065	.401	.135	.450	.019	.263
Complexities in operations	.099	.129	-.042	-.152	.486	-.431	.378	-.042	-.232	.146
Lack of inter exchange competition	.324	.112	-.261	-.335	-.308	.103	.333	.151	-.119	-.397
Limited revenue	-.144	.621	.142	.157	.318	.089	-.010	.196	.181	-.173
Inequitable burden sharing	.155	.574	.214	.057	-.415	.089	-.127	.083	.017	.165
Low level of capital expenditure	.223	-.357	-.223	-.418	-.130	-.132	-.247	.045	.176	.301
No financial guarantee	.328	.447	.211	.248	-.254	.255	-.129	-.087	-.043	.159
Few professional	.256	-.139	-.215	.098	.316	.147	-.106	-.519	-.043	-.020
Lack of training and development	.290	.228	-.572	-.041	-.226	.314	.157	-.053	.050	-.071
Inability to develop new products and services	.309	.192	-.490	-.129	.085	.139	-.162	-.156	-.109	.452

(Contd.)

TABLE 2.19 *(Contd.)*

1	*2*	*3*	*4*	*5*	*6*	*7*	*8*	*9*	*10*	*11*
Low levels of actual settlement	.357	-.270	.189	.009	.176	.395	-.127	-.139	.316	-.261
Concentration of liquidity and market capitalization	.396	-.184	.292	.165	.282	.386	-.085	-.113	-.325	-.012
Dominance of badla financing	.434	-.073	-.082	-.500	.178	-.003	.213	-.141	.345	-.174
Excessive volatility	.198	.294	.191	-.383	.427	.047	.286	.280	.142	.171
Weak criteria to become a member	.313	.068	-.115	.392	.206	-.065	-.148	.216	.421	-.052
Weak criteria to become a broker	.197	-.160	.136	.448	-.215	-.174	.522	.062	.216	.041
Weak criteria to become a market maker	.182	-.180	-.058	.653	.081	-.082	.288	-.151	.170	.151
Barrier to entry of new intermediaries	.508	.294	-.129	.213	.132	-.301	-.200	-.294	.065	-.031
Membership card treated as investment instrument	.389	.075	.450	.031	-.308	-.225	-.164	.011	-.066	-.092
Low capitalization of brokers	.494	.484	.113	-.237	.070	-.023	.026	.030	-.153	-.132
A single class of brokers	.075	.021	.338	-.068	.361	-.025	-.357	.328	.111	.091

Extraction Method: Principal Component Analysis.
a: 10 components extracted.

TABLE 2.20

Rotated Component Matrix(b)

	Component									
	1	2	3	4	5	6	7	8	9	10
1	2	3	4	5	6	7	8	9	10	11
Ineffective regulation of members	-.133	.106	-.144	-.128	.101	.049	.125	.808	-.011	-.053
Ineffective regulation of listed companies	.020	.550	.123	.103	.379	-.015	-.064	.333	.163	-.180
Unequal access to corporate announcements	.236	.252	.173	-.012	.200	.025	.026	-.405	-.468	.069
Non-performance of outside directors (non-member directors)	.195	.680	.076	.228	.015	-.064	.067	.109	-.166	.220
Division of liquidity and distortion of price discovery	-.052	.033	.017	.167	.751	-.088	.042	.038	.075	.055
Cost inefficiency for all stakeholders	.061	.163	.059	.119	.250	-.067	.134	.005	.706	.065
Complexities in operations	-.257	-.007	.590	.114	.082	.191	-.026	.019	-.198	-.428
Lack of inter-exchange competition	.065	.111	.176	-.105	.066	-.164	.776	.120	.039	.043
Limited revenue	.260	-.622	.331	-.012	-.154	-.104	-.157	.183	.020	.067
Inequitable burden sharing	.761	-.055	.007	-.045	-.141	-.101	.042	-.071	.050	-.093
Low level of capital expenditure	-.135	.675	.025	-.199	-.203	.119	-.035	-.018	.204	.089
No financial guarantee	.728	-.100	-.050	.076	.115	.149	.012	-.068	.067	.042
Few professionals	-.153	-.018	-.056	.036	.171	.661	.028	.029	-.086	.204
Lack of training and development	.151	-.043	-.022	.013	-.115	.284	.615	.088	.375	.055
Inability to develop new products and services	.150	.173	.107	-.175	-.077	.616	.089	-.002	.400	-.186

(Contd.)

TABLE 2.20 *(Contd.)*

1	*2*	*3*	*4*	*5*	*6*	*7*	*8*	*9*	*10*	*11*
Low levels of actual settlement	-.009	.050	.025	.048	.243	.132	-.012	.010	-.003	.738
Concentration of liquidity and market capitalization	.112	-.019	.030	-.028	.714	.246	-.125	-.048	-.006	.233
Dominance of badla financing	-.154	.279	.504	-.020	-.111	.169	.332	-.038	-.088	.424
Excessive volatility	.046	-.062	.797	-.076	.018	-.081	-.061	-.147	.148	.050
Weak criteria to become a member	.125	-.029	.127	.369	-.098	.090	-.195	.457	.225	.282
Weak criteria to become a broker	.048	.100	-.005	.779	.077	-.204	.116	-.068	-.014	-.017
Weak criteria to become a market maker	-.049	-.044	-.120	.753	.125	.219	-.098	.039	.074	-.005
Barrier to entry of new intermediaries	.318	.095	.158	.200	-.071	.513	-.009	.394	-.220	.011
Membership card treated as investment instrument	.491	.319	.012	.062	.160	-.171	-.044	.107	-.355	.067
Low capitalization of brokers	.442	.005	.484	-.169	.136	.113	.243	.157	-.145	-.001
A single class of brokers	.092	.041	.288	-.194	.099	-.141	-.533	.170	.061	.186

Extraction Method: Principal Component Analysis. Rotation Method: Varimax with Kaiser Normalization.
a: Rotation converged in 18 iterations.

TABLE 2.21

Component Transformation Matrix

Component	*1*	2	3	4	5	6	7	8	9	*10*
1	.398	.484	.352	.212	.366	.323	.242	.275	.049	.252
2	.634	-.517	.344	-.135	-.322	.102	.119	.085	-.039	-.238
3	.334	-.007	.149	.045	.318	-.415	-.438	-.362	-.470	.218
4	.169	-.346	-.427	.671	.214	.088	-.254	.292	.095	.086
5	-.441	-.345	.550	-.054	.218	.342	-.421	.172	.013	.099
6	.132	.361	-.177	-.236	.337	.085	.176	-.369	.510	.466
7	-.245	-.164	.365	.536	.110	-.189	.489	-.408	.001	-.201
8	.028	.055	.242	-.062	.109	-.687	-.111	.368	.538	-.114
9	-.013	.042	.141	.353	-.649	-.073	-.139	-.035	.139	.623
10	.162	.312	.088	.105	-.101	.263	-.438	-.483	.444	-.395

Extraction Method: Principal Component Analysis.
Rotation Method: Varimax with Kaiser Normalization.

level of actual settlement. The respondents are of the opinion that low level of capital expenditure on infrastructure by the RSEs taken together with low level of actual settlement are least contributing factors towards economic efficiency of the exchanges.

The respondents felt that there is a need to consolidate the regional stock exchanges into one bigger exchange in order to compete with other two big exchanges like NSE and BSE. They further felt that the Indo Next exchange should be made independent of BSE, and, if that is not possible, then the other remaining regional exchanges should be given a mandate to form a third bigger consolidated exchange.

3.4 CONCLUSION

After going through the major developments as a part of this study, to analyze the performance evaluation of the regional stock exchanges it can be safely concluded that the regional stock exchanges contributed immensely towards raising the capital resources by tapping the primary market. There has been 2.5 times increase in amount raised from the primary market during the last 15 years. However, the decline in the business of regional stock exchanges as a part of secondary market function can be attributed to various reasons.

The first and major is the establishment of National Stock exchange (NSE) in 1994 with an all India spread throughout the country and expansion of operations of Bombay Stock Exchange (BSE), both of which have their trader work stations at over 400 centers in the country today, have led to virtual extinction of all the 19 regional stock exchanges spread across the length and breadth of the country. The share of 19 RSEs, which was as much as 5.6 per cent of the total all India turnover of Rs. 2.39 lakh crore in 1995-96, declined progressively year after year and in 2001-02 it was just 8.4 per cent of the total volume of Rs. 8.96 lakh crore. At present, there is virtually no trading at any of these RSEs.

Secondly, Abolition of Badla with effect from July, 2001 which acted as backbone of trading at Calcutta, Delhi,

Ahmedabad and Ludhiana Stock Exchanges and also at a few other exchanges dealt a serious blow to trading at the RSEs.

The practice of badla provided an opportunity to the speculators and the brokers to carry over the outstanding exposure at the end of one settlement period to the next settlement period by paying carry over charges. This was an easy way of financing the purchase of the securities and keeping them over a longer period of time. This was a common practice on regional exchanges which led to considerable increase in the turnover as financing was arranged by the exchange brokers and was an easy option.

Thirdly, introduction of uniform trading cycles at all the stock exchanges reduced further the volume of trading at these exchanges due to diminished opportunities for arbitrage transactions.

The regional stock exchanges had different trading cycles or periods which provided an arbitrage opportunity to the speculators and brokers to take advantage of the price difference of a security being traded at two different exchanges. This reduced the market risk as whenever the market spread provided any opportunity to gain the speculator or the broker would take advantage of this opportunity by buying at a low price and selling at high price at two different exchanges.

Fourthly, introduction of the compulsory rolling settlements on a T+5 basis accelerated the reduction in turnover at the RSEs. The switch over of the rolling settlement to T+3 effective from 2002 and to T+2 from 2003 virtually sealed the fate of the regional stock exchanges.

Rolling settlement is a method of ensuring timely closure and honour of deals. The rolling settlement mode requires positions to be closed compulsorily at the end of each trading day. With introduction of rolling settlement the speculative turnover has reduced considerably as now the speculator or the broker is required to square up the deal before the end of the trading session or otherwise make arrangement for buying the scrip or release the delivery as the case may be if he is a seller. This has also effected the short selling in the market because the single trading day does not provide enough or lucrative opportunity to short sell a scrip.

Fifthly, yet another major reason for the absence of trading at the RSEs is that all the major operators in these exchanges acquired membership of either NSE or BSE or of both, while the smaller brokers acquired sub-brokership of members of NSE/BSE and all of them switched over their operations completely to NSE or BSE.

Sixthly, the last nail into the coffin of the RSEs was drawn by the Ministry of Finance in 2003, by withdrawing its earlier circulars which required the companies including the existing listed companies to be listed on the regional stock exchange in the state where the registered office of the company is situated. The withdrawal of this circular had an effect as to loss of one of the significant revenue generating activity of these RSEs by way of receiving the listing fees from such listed companies annually. The Companies now delisted themselves from the regional exchanges and listed on NSE or BSE.

As such all the activities of the RSEs are brought to a halt and the exchanges have no business transacted and are virtually defunct with a huge infrastructure base, which at once was the backbone of financial sector, lying waste and of no use.

Further factor analysis reveals that maximum factor loading of .801 is given to lack of market education and minimum factor loading is in case of inadequate growth of unit holders. A large number of respondents feel that lack or inadequate market knowledge or education has been the main factor responsible for inadequate growth of RSEs.

The maximum factor loading of .786 was observed in lack of inter-exchange competition. The respondents feel that RSEs have not been able to provide enough opportunities for the investors as well the brokers to compete amongst each other.

The respondents felt that there is a need to consolidate the regional stock exchanges into one bigger exchange in order to compete with other two big exchanges like NSE and BSE. They further felt that the Indo Next exchange should be made independent of BSE and if that is not possible then or the other remaining regional exchanges should be given a mandate to form a third bigger consolidated exchange.

The study also reveals that the regional stock exchanges have not played adequate role in promoting the equity cult in the region. They have not been able to play any major role in managing the non-traded, thinly traded or marginally traded shares. There have been three reasons identified from the secondary survey for lack of liquidity in the stock exchanges. First, the equity base of the listed stocks of a large number of companies is quite low. Secondly, the floating stock of listed securities, particularly those held by the public, is quite low. Third, there are no market-makers or specialists, as in almost all the developed markets.

The respondents also felt that in case regional exchanges are to be revived, than the regional companies whose shares were listed earlier on these exchanges should be given priority in re-listing by way of one time waiver of the listing fees. Further, they also suggested and opined on the issue of the management of thinly traded or marginally traded scrips by introducing the concept of specialist or market-makers, introducing call auction system, increasing the minimum public holding, making mandatory the role of market-makers or specialists in case of new or initial public offers.

Note and Reference

1. Gupta Renu (2002), *op. cit.*

REVIVAL STRATEGIES OF RSEs

In this chapter the revival of regional stock exchanges, through diversification of their business and re-organization or restructuring is discussed. The analysis is based on the secondary data collected from various annual reports of these exchanges, websites, internet, magazines, journals and libraries. The study was supplemented with primary data collected by canvassing questionnaire-*cum*-opinion survey. Factor analysis has also been used to highlight the importance of dominating factors responsible for revival of regional exchanges by resorting to diversification and reorganization of the business activities. The emerging trends in the form of alternative models of future stock exchanges have also been discussed in this chapter.

3.1 STRATEGY AND REVIVAL STRATEGIES

The word strategy is defined as the direction and scope of an organization over the long-term: which achieves advantage for the organization through its configuration of resources within a changing environment, to meet the needs of markets and to fulfil stakeholder expectations.[1]

Strategy becomes a fundamental framework through which an organization can assert its vital continuity, while at the same time purposefully managing its adaptation to the changing environment to gain competitive advantage. Strategy includes the formal recognition that the recipients of the results of a firm's actions are the wide constituency of its stakeholders.

Therefore, the ultimate objective of strategy is to address stakeholder benefits to provide a base for establishing the host of transactions and social contracts that link a firm to its stakeholders.[2]

Apart from the three generic strategies as profounded by Michael E. Porter the growth and revival strategies of a firm include the diversification and reorganizing or restructuring strategies.[3] Diversification involves organizations moving into new product and market activities.

Diversification can be divided into two categories, i.e. related and unrelated. Related diversification involves moving into activities that have some degree of relationship with current activities—forming part of the same broad value system. Backward integration means moving into related supply activities. Forward integration means moving into activities closer to the final customer, such as brewers moving into the management of pubs. Horizontal integration means moving into complimentary or competitive activities, Honda makes cars and motorcycles. Unrelated diversification implies moving into new product and market activities that have little direct link with current activities. At the extreme end of the spectrum is conglomerate diversification where there is no direct relationship between the existing business and the new activities.

The reorganization or restructuring strategies include, apart from financial restructuring, the restructuring of organization structure as independent SBUs and reorganizing the activities of the organization in order to revive a sick or fail business and making it viable.

Indian securities market has a large number of stocks. With the recent reforms in the securities markets, regional stock exchanges have lost their business, making it harder for them to provide the liquidity. How to overcome this problem has been engaging the attention of regulators and the national level stock exchanges. With all the RSEs having already virtually grounded to a halt and with the growing illiquidity at the NSE and BSE in respect of a vast number of shares, it is imperative that a solution needs to be evolved in the larger interest of millions of investors of the country.

The revival strategies of RSEs have been discussed under Diversification and Re-organization of RSEs.

3.2 DIVERSIFICATION OF BUSINESS OF RSEs

The traditional role of regional stock exchanges can be listed as raising capital for businesses, mobilizing savings for investment, facilitating company growth, redistribution of wealth, creating investment opportunities for small investors and providing market for trading of securities which are listed on these particular regional exchanges.

However, the regional stock exchanges are out of business or closed because of various reasons and there is a need to look into revival of stock exchanges through diversification in their line of businesses.

The survey conducted reveals that about sixty-seven per cent respondents were of the opinion that they seek revival of the regional exchanges. The remaining 33 per cent respondents opined that they are not in the favour of the revival of the regional exchanges (Table 3.1)

TABLE 3.1

Response towards Revival of RSEs

(N=105)

Sr. No.	Particular	Response	Number	Per centage
1.	Do you seek revival?	Yes	70	66.67
2.	Do you seek revival?	No	35	33.33

A scrutiny of the data further reveals that majority of the respondents (66.67 per cent) favoured the revival of regional stock exchanges. The respondents felt that huge infrastructure has been created by the regional exchanges which is presently lying idle or waste. The revival strategies or model may use the infrastructure or expertise of these exchanges to diversify into other areas of business. A large majority of them further suggested that the regional stock exchanges should consolidate to form a bigger exchange. They also opined that Indo Next Exchange should be handed over to the regional exchanges and should be kept outside the purview of BSE.

The respondents were also of the opinion that regional stock exchanges should also have a tie-up with large exchanges. They however felt that the issue of control and interest of the regional and small investor should be taken care of by the large exchange prior to any such tie-up. This issue if further probed in the subsequent analysis.

However, 33.33 per cent of respondents were of the opinion that there is no need to revive the regional exchanges since they are unlikely to serve the purpose for which they were created. They feel that the national exchanges NSE and BSE are providing better alternatives to the investors for trading and were more transparent in conduct of business and had a wide reach through screen-based trading.

Further, when asked as to whether the respondents were aware of the revival strategies, if any, adopted by RSEs in other developed nations having robust capital markets the responses are contained in Table 3.2. The responses shows that majority (73 per cent) of the respondents were not aware of the revival solutions adopted by RSEs in other nations. Most of them were even ignorant about the status of the regional exchanges in other countries. The respondents were only aware about the presence of major stock exchanges in the world.

In contrast a small number (27 per cent) of the respondents were aware of the revival strategies or solutions related to RSEs in other nations. They were aware about the Euro Next exchange which is conceived as a consolidated effort to bring together the regional exchanges of Europe. These respondents also favoured the concept of specialized exchanges, as in USA. The respondents also echoed some areas of concern related to revival of regional exchanges like adopting a sustainable business model, looking into regional aspirations of the investors and entrepreneurs, identifying and diversifying into new areas of business and emerging as specialized exchanges of that region.

TABLE 3.2

Awareness of the Revival Solutions Adopted by RSEs in Other Nations

(N=105)

Sr. No.	*Response*	*Number*	*Per centage*
1.	Yes	28	27
2.	No	77	73

The survey (Table 3.3) also reveals that majority (89.52 per cent) of the respondents were aware of the revival initiatives adopted by SEBI and only a few (10.48 per cent) were not aware of the same.

TABLE 3.3

Awareness of Initiatives taken by SEBI for Revival of the RSEs

(N=105)

Sr. No.	*Response*	*Number*	*Per centage*
1.	Yes	94	89.52
2.	No	11	10.48

The respondents who were aware of the revival alternatives provided by the regulator however were highly skeptical about the success of these alternatives and felt that SEBI should play a more dynamic and positive role in reviving the regional exchanges.

The sixty seven per cent of the respondents who had favoured revival of the regional stock exchanges, opined that diversification and reorganization can be used as strategies to revive them (Table 3.4).

TABLE 3.4

Response towards Modes of Revival

(N = 70)

Sr. No.	*Response*	*Number*	*Per centage*
1.	Diversification	49	70.00
2.	Reorganization	21	30.00

Table 3.4 shows that seventy per cent of the respondents favoured the revival through the mode of diversification of business of these regional stock exchanges and thirty per cent were of the opinion that revival should be undertaken through the mode of reorganization. Diversification of activities would imply that the regional exchanges could undertake or open up for conducting other allied businesses and reorganization would mean, restructuring the present organization of the regional exchanges so as to make them more efficient. The respondents who were seeking revival of regional exchanges through re-organization strategy were of the opinion that regional stock exchanges should have a tie-up with large exchanges or they should merge to form an independent exchange. However, the opinion towards consolidation of regional exchanges towards forming a large exchange was more stronger.

3.2.1 Diversification of RSEs

The respondents in the survey who sought to revive the regional exchanges were asked to rank in order of preference the various business opportunities recorded in the questionnaire and their responses are tabulated, their weighted averages were computed and were ranked on the basis of computed weighted averages. These are given in Table 3.5.

TABLE 3.5

Diversification Activities of RSEs

Sr. No.	Areas of Operation for diversification and new businesses	Weighted Avg.	Rank
1.	Portfolio Management Services	13.22	1
2.	Commodities Trading	12.49	2
3.	Marketing of investment products	10.73	3
4.	Merchant/Investment Banking	8.89	4
5.	Operating as regional centers of NSE/BSE	8.87	5
6.	Investor Education and Courses	8.56	6
7.	Providing Dematerialization Services	8.40	7
8.	Operating as regional center of SEBI	8.27	8
9.	Foreign Exchange Trading/SME trading	7.33	9

I. Portfolio Management Services

Portfolio management services relate to extended specialized services provided to the investor by constructing and managing an efficient portfolio of the investor. Efficient portfolio aims to maximize the returns and minimize the risk. The brokers and the regional exchange can develop this in-house service for the benefit of the clients or investors by charging an additional fee and guiding the investors as to buying and selling of securities. Presently this service is provided by banks through their broking division or arm, specialized corporate brokers, institutions, mutual funds and so on.

The survey results reveal that the respondents with a weighted average mean score of 13.22 ranked at number 1 position introduction of portfolio management services as an area of diversification for regional stock exchanges and felt that the stock exchanges should diversify and provide this specialist service to the investors of the region. The exchange can develop this service by recruiting specialists who are trained to carry such activities. The regional exchanges already have the required infrastructure including the hardware and software, specialist information on any scrip, library research and so on for managing such activity.

2. Commodities Trading

Commodity trading has already been introduced in India by setting up of specialized commodity exchanges namely, NCDEX and MCX.. The National Commodities Derivatives Exchange of India and Multi-Commodity Exchange are both based in Mumbai and deal in agro commodities and bullion trading. These commodity exchanges provide opportunities for trading in the form of futures and options. The various agro commodities including oilseeds listed for trading include wheat, rice, soyabean, sarson, gur, mentha oil, etc. It also includes industrial metals such as copper, aluminium, iron and so on apart from precious metals like gold and silver.

The respondents with a weighted average mean score of 12.49 ranked at number 2 position commodities trading as a good business option available to revive the regional exchanges. The regional exchanges have already been given one time waiver to become member of both NCDEX and MCX via subsidiary route. The regional stock exchanges have already started providing the services of commodity trading to the investors in the region through their existing brokers. The regional exchanges have formed their subsidiary company to be member of these specialized exchanges and through its subsidiary the regional exchange is conducting all commodities related trading activities.

3. Marketing of Investment Products

The various investment and financial products are presently marketed by banks, insurance companies, mutual funds, corporate broking houses, finance companies, etc. The issuer of these products mostly gives the right to sell and promote these products to a third party in lieu of a handsome fixed commission. This has also led to Bancassurance whereby many banks are selling third party insurance to its customers and earning handsome returns.

The survey reveals that respondents with a weighted average mean score of 10.73 ranked at number 3 position marketing of investment products as a lucrative business option available to revive the regional exchanges. The regional stock exchanges have largest registered data base in terms of the investors in the region. These investors are clients to one or many brokers of these exchanges and further invest their savings into securities market with the advice of the brokers. The brokers influence a lot as opinion leaders for making investment. These brokers can generate lots of business for the exchange through their clients or investors by selling insurance, banking term deposits, mutual fund schemes and so on as to add to the business volume and returns of the regional stock exchange.

4. Merchant/Investment Banking

This refers to group of all such activities which involve managing the complete IPO or preparing the company for a public issue. The role of a merchant banker is to ensure that all necessary compliances of statutory authorities have been met by the company and they further undertake to carry out the public issue and are involved in selling and promotion of the same to the underwriters, brokers, financial institutions, overseas corporate bodies and general public.

The respondents with a weighted average mean score of 8.89 ranked at number 4 position merchant or investment banking as a business option which can be added to the portfolio of the regional exchanges. The regional exchanges have all the necessary infrastructure required to carry on the activities of merchant banking. They can further recruit specialist professionals who can help or manage in carrying out these activities for the exchanges. In fact, the regional stock exchanges can be one stop shops or partners for local entrepreneurs those to wish to tap the primary market and raise funds for their expansions, upcoming projects, diversification activities, etc. All what is required from the promoters is to file an application with the exchange and rest everything can be taken care of by the regional stock exchanges.

5. Regional Centers of NSE and BSE

The regional stock exchanges can represent the regional interest of the investors and entrepreneurs by operating as regional centers of the large exchanges like NSE and BSE. These centers can carry activities on behalf of the bigger exchanges. They can represent the regional trading interest of the brokers, investors by providing all relevant information, carry investor education activities on behalf of NSE or BSE. These regional centers can also provide all necessary information to the entrepreneurs of the region who wish to come out with a public issue to raise equity from the market.

The survey reveals that respondents with a weighted average mean score of 8.87 at number 5 position felt that the regional stock exchanges can open regional centers of bigger exchanges like NSE or BSE and charge fee from the bigger exchanges while extending services to investors, brokers and entrepreneurs in the region while representing the interest of these exchanges. The regional stock exchanges through their subsidiaries are already members of these two bigger exchanges. The regional exchanges can represent the interests of investor and entrepreneur of the region in which they are located by becoming centers of NSE or BSE.

6. Investor Education and Courses

The investors required to be made aware of the general conditions prevailing in the economy and the techniques used for buying and selling the shares. The general investor needs to understand the intricacies of the stock markets and understand the fundamental analysis and technical analysis used for buying and selling the scrip. The regional stock exchanges can provide excellent platform to educate the investor by conducting relevant workshops in the region to provide insight about the stock market operations to the investor. The investors and other traders can benefit from such education a lot where presently they rely on the broker's advice and market rumors heavily thereby losing money.

The respondents with a weighted average mean score of 8.56 at number 6 position felt that regional exchanges should enter into providing investor education and appropriate courses related to it. These courses can be for beginners level and also high end courses may be designed for building expertise into trading strategies. The need for investor education and relevant courses has been felt more after the introduction of derivatives trading in India for which the investors have little knowledge and expertise as to how they can effectively make use of options and futures for minimizing their risk.

7. Providing Dematerialization Services

The trading settlement system of the stock exchanges was not efficient in India due to the time taken for settlement and due to the physical movement of paper form of securities. Further, the transfer of shares in favour of the buyer by the company also consumed considerable amount of time. To obviate these problems, the Depositories Act, 1996 was passed to provide for the establishment of depositories in securities with the objective of ensuring free transferability of securities with speed and accuracy. Dematerilisation is the process of converting the paper form of security into electronic form for easy transferability and doing away with the bad delivery of shares. This act brought in changes by: (a) making securities of public limited companies freely transferable subject to certain exceptions; (b) dematerialising of securities in the depository mode. In order to promote dematerialisation, the regulator has been promoting settlement in demat form in a phased manner in an ever-increasing number of securities. The stamp duty on transfer of demat securities has been waived. There are two depositories in India, viz. NSDL and CDSL. They have been set-up to provide instantaneous electronic transfer of securities.

The survey reveals that respondents with a weighted average mean score of 8.40 at number 7 position were of the opinion that the regional stock exchanges should become the depository participant with any of the two depositories or both and start demat services. This would not only help in generating income for the stock exchange but also facilitate the investor as these regional exchanges would become one-stop shops wherein apart from trading the investor can also open the demat account and enjoy these services under the same roof which shall be more convenient to him with respect to time and management of his account.

8. Operating as Regional Centers of SEBI

Securities and Exchange Board of India which is the

market regulator is having its headquarters in Mumbai and regional offices in Delhi, Chennai and Kolkata. The infrastructure of the 19 regional exchanges can be used for opening the regional centers of SEBI for the dual purpose of playing the developmental and regulatory role. The aspect of investor grievance handling shall become more effective and at the same time the watch dog can have more efficient and effective control on the activities of entire trading community and other market makers by being near to them. Rather than playing the role of doing the postmortem on certain happening in capital markets, SEBI can enlarge its vigil on the market players by let the regional exchanges become its regional centers. Other activities related to investor education and broker education can be effectively implemented.

The respondents with a weighted average mean score of 8.27 at number 8 position felt the need for regional exchanges to operate as regional centre of SEBI. The respondents were of this view as they felt that by doing this the investor's grievance and complaints redressal process shall get a boost as the investors shall only be needed to make a complaint to the official of SEBI who would be available all time at the regional exchange. This would hasten up the complaint redressal. At the same time the respondents felt that brokers and other intermediaries shall also effectively function as the presence of SEBI officials shall make them improve their functioning and the market regulator shall be able to effectively enlarge its vigil in the functioning of the capital markets, both primary and secondary by having its presence in these regional exchanges. A regional officer may be appointed by SEBI to head its presence in these regional exchanges.

9. Foreign Exchange Trading/SME Trading

Foreign Exchange trading is another area where the regional exchanges can look for business. At present there are various banks or private players which are facilitating these services. The regional exchanges by effectively entering into forex trading can provide opportunities to its brokers to trade on behalf of their clients. At the same time the regional exchanges can enable the export houses or export-oriented units or importing entity to buy, sell or hedge its foreign exchange requirement on these exchanges. Small and medium enterprises is another area where the regional exchanges can play an all important role by helping these entrepreneurs to raise capital from the market and provide specialized exchange for SME trading.

The survey reveals that respondents with a weighted average mean score of 7.33 at number 9 position opined that the regional exchanges must diversify into forex trading and SME trading. They felt that it would provide business opportunity to the brokers of these exchanges on one hand and shall provide an opportunity to the regional small and medium entrepreneur to raise capital but also look into his foreign exchange requirement by ways of trading on these exchanges. The regional investor as well as the industry would be facilitated when the regional exchanges shall start providing these services.

3.3 REORGANIZATION OF RSEs

Considering that the RSEs had invested substantially in the infrastructure, which included buildings, hardware and software for automated trading, several initiatives were taken to revive these exchanges so that the infrastructure could be put to productive use.

Securities and Exchange Board of India, the apex regulatory body which has been dealing with this problem of revival of regional stock exchanges has provided many alternatives during the recent past. The first among them was the setting up of the ICSE platform, to regroup the RSEs to provide a third national market. The ICSE was promoted in 1998 by 14 RSEs for providing an additional trading platform where the shares listed on any of these 14 exchanges would be traded. The ICSE was thus conceptualized as a stock exchange to provide a common trading platform to members of all participating stock exchanges, mainly with the objective of boosting trade in the securities listed on the participating stock exchanges. It was felt that such trading across different stock exchanges would generate renewed trading interest among investors by providing them an opportunity to trade in large number of shares that were listed on the participating exchanges. However, this could not materialise. The existing regional order books of the participating exchanges continued. This fragmented the order book and thus depleted the liquidity in the shares exclusively listed and traded on the RSEs. On account of lack of liquidity, ICSE did not succeed.

The second effort was to permit the RSEs to set-up broking subsidiaries which could pool the financial resources of regional brokers and of the exchanges and obtain membership of the BSE and NSE. The regional brokers could then act as sub-brokers to the subsidiaries which had registered as brokers and have access to the markets of BSE and NSE. Even the ICSE set-up such a broking subsidiary. Though the scheme maintained the purity of the functions of the exchanges, most subsidiaries became successful brokers in the market of other exchange(s). Although the subsidiaries were basically brokers, there were several differences between them and corporate broking firms, primarily because these were subsidiaries of the stock exchanges.

The third effort was when SEBI took the initiative to encourage the BSE and the smaller stock exchanges to set-up the BSE Indo Next trading platform as a separate trading platform under the present BOLT trading system of the BSE. It was a joint initiative of the BSE and the Federation of Indian Stock Exchanges (FISE) of which 18 RSEs are members. The BSE Indo Next market was intended to be an SME specific market. The BSE Indo Next trading platform was supposed to be implemented in phases. But it has not yet started.

This research study appraises itself of the present status of the RSEs in the light of the discussions with senior functionaries and exchange officials of three RSEs namely Delhi, Ludhiana and Jaipur exchanges.

The RSEs were established with the objective of providing a regional market for raising capital by companies at the regional level by garnering regional savings to help achieve a balanced regional development and to spread the equity cult among investors in the country. This objective has been fairly served by the RSEs for a length of time. But with the advent of modern telecommunication and information technology and the symbiotic interaction of technology and the markets, which facilitated a fundamental transformation of the market micro-structure, the scope of the RSEs became limited till they virtually lost their relevance.

The present research study also recognizes that even internationally, and precisely for similar reasons, the RSEs have had a chequered past and over a very short period of time became moribund before the burgeoning growth of the national stock exchanges with national and international reach. This prompted a move towards consolidation of RSEs.

The above situation naturally raises the basic question on the raison d'être of the RSEs and their subsidiaries in the present market structure. When this question was posed before the RSEs, it did not evince any convincing response. They did not come with any specific viable business plan for the revival of the RSEs excepting pinning hopes on a future which might be bright. The study also notes that there are certain deeply embedded behavioural issues which continue to dominate the mind set of the members of the RSEs and they seem to be coming in the way of some of the RSEs accepting the reality which demands sub-ordination of their individual and independent identity before the larger interest of the very survival of the RSEs. Indeed, it was this attitude, coupled with the equally uncompromising attitude of the business partners, which was responsible for the failure of the various rehabilitatory measures taken in the past for the revival of the RSEs. Equally, the members of the RSEs, by virtue of their access to national trading platforms through the subsidiary route did not find any incentive to trade and promote trading in the RSEs.

There have also been serious regulatory concerns from time to time on the functioning of some of the RSEs. These regulatory concerns had led SEBI to take recourse to the extreme measure of superseding the governing boards of some exchanges and even to withdraw the recognition in the case of four regional exchanges.

Although the RSEs have ceased to perform the basic economic function for which they were set-up, their continued existence by itself, necessitates regular onsite and offsite regulatory monitoring and surveillance. Regulatory resources are thus thinly spread and the attention of the regulator is diverted from more emergent issues to grappling with such routine issues which relate to dysfunctional entities.

It is thus clear that any solution to the conundrum posed by the RSEs must encompass all the issues delineated above including the deeply embedded behavioural issues. Equally, such solutions must not only be practicable and implementable but also eschew adhocism and discretion which had informed and also thwarted some of the past initiatives for revival of the RSEs.

The re-organizing of these RSEs may involve revival of the RSEs through any or combination of these, firstly revival through restructuring of the RSEs by demutualization of these exchanges, secondly allowing for the divestment of the stake of the demutualised/corporatised exchange, thirdly by allowing the regional exchanges to form a single consolidated entity to compete with the other two bigger exchanges like NSE and BSE and fourthly providing exit route for the RSEs which desire withdrawal of recognition.

3.3.1 Demutualization of Regional Stock Exchanges

Traditionally most of the stock exchanges have been non-profit and mutual or cooperative organization all over the world. Their precise legal form varied from country to country, depending upon the domestic legal and corporate finance system, but their ownership and governance structure has some common features.

In India, most of the exchanges are organized as "Association of person" under Section 25 of Companies Act, 1956. These exchanges are "mutual" exchanges and these are non-profit organization and exempted from tax. The stock exchanges used generally to be owned, controlled and governed by exchange members who are usually stock brokers. Brokers elect their representatives to regulate the activities of exchange including their own activities. On one side trading members are owner of the stock exchanges and on the other side they are consumers or they are real beneficiaries. In mutual exchange ownership, management and trading is in same hands. Now this traditional ownership and governance structure is being questioned. In mutilated organization there is always conflict between regulatory and public interest role of exchange with private interest of elected directors. The main reasons are scams by exchange management.

Largely due to the brokers interference with day-to-day administration and ultimate decision-making power is in hands of brokers due to absence of SEBI nominees and public representatives in board meeting. The limitations of mutualized structure give birth to the demutualized structure.

Concept of Demutulization

The concept of Demutualization broadly means the separation of ownership from the management so that, conflict of interest could be avoided and the exchanges could behave as a for profit organization.

Thus Demutualization is a process whereby a mutual company becomes a stock (share) company. A mutual company belongs to its voting policy-holders, whereas a stock company is owned by its shareholders. In other words, it is a process by which mutual organizations or companies (mutuals) convert themselves to for-profit (or profit-making) public companies which distribute profits to their shareholders in the form of dividends.

Demutualization usually involves the sale or reorganization of a mutual entity, by its members, to or into a non-mutual company whose shares can be traded on a stock market. This maneuver generally improves the company's access to investment capital, and so increases its value as a viable business.

Demutualization was originally used to refer specifically to this conversion process by insurance companies; the term has since become more broadly used to describe the process by which any member-owned organization becomes shareholder-owned. Worldwide, stock exchanges have offered another striking example of the trend towards demutualization, as the London Stock Exchange (LSE), New York Stock Exchange (NYSE), Toronto Stock Exchange (TSE) and most other exchanges across the globe have either recently converted, are currently in the process, or are considering demutualization.

Reasons for Demutualization

I. Conflict between interest of investors and brokers.

Conflict between the interest of investors and brokers is main drawback of mutual exchange. The elected directors misuse their official positions for personal interest. In case of dispute between brokers and investors, investor's interest do not always receive the same utmost objective treatment. The regulatory and public interest role of the exchange conflict with private interest of the elected directors as the same sometime gets precedence over regulation broker on exchange does not offer an effective model for self-regulatory organization.

2. Absence of SEBI Nominees and public representative in board meetings

Many non-broker directors are busy in their professional life, they do not often understand the intricacies of functioning of stock exchanges and are not assertive enough and not regular in attending meetings.

So in board meetings broker-director have dominance over taking important decisions. Mutualized exchanges lack quality of administration or we can say broker managed exchanges is far from satisfactory stage where ultimate owners and real beneficiaries are same.

3. Lack of adequate funds

Today where stock market needs change for technological advancement, mutual exchanges have no funds of which most of the part they got from members. For further expansion, these exchanges need funds, which these can collect from commercialization of stock exchanges.

So mutualized exchanges are facing so many problems. These exchanges want their own place among the crowd. These need differentiation. The only solution for problem of mutual structure is demutual structure.

4. Conflict between elected broker and others

Another major drawback of mutualized stock exchange is that there is conflict between elected broker and others.

The elected brokers misuse their official position for personal interest.

5. Lack of Professional Management

The mutualized stock exchange lacks professional management because of conflict between brokers and investors.

6. Low public confidence

Due to lack of professional management and lack of transparency public lack confidence in stock exchange and resist to invest.

7. Lack of Transparency

Mutualized stock exchange lacks transparency as they do not reveal the full information as required by brokers and investors.

Demutualization in India

The accepted norms of behaviour of members and their self-imposed rules for trading governed the stock markets of the country. Members were responsible for their conduct with one another, with users of the exchange and other stakeholders. With securities law in place, the concept of self-regulation under regulatory oversight emerged. But conflict of interest between members being owners of the Exchanges and also in the management of the Stock Exchanges persisted, which led to the concept of demutualization. Further, the experience of demutualized Exchanges has been positive and praise worthy leading to emergence of this concept. SEBI taking a cue from this, set-up a committee under the chairmanship of Justice M.H. Kania to study, suggest about corporatisation and demutualization of Indian stock exchanges in 2002.

Historically, brokers owned, controlled and managed the stock exchanges. In case of disputes, the integrity of the exchange suffered. Therefore, regulators focused on reducing the dominance of brokers in the management of stock exchanges. They advised them to reconstitute their governing boards to provide for at least 50 per cent non-broker representation. However, this did not materially alter the situation. In face of extreme volatility in the securities market in 2000, the Government proposed to Corporatise and Demutualize the Stock Exchanges by which ownership, management and trading membership would be segregated from one another. The Stock Exchanges in India stand demutualized.

The primary survey (Table 3.6) reveals that only forty one per cent of the brokers of the regional exchanges were in the favour of Demutualization and subsequently offering an IPO to the investing public to augment their financial resources for the growth of the business activities at the exchanges. The remaining fifty nine per cent were not in favour of the Demutualization Scheme and were satisfied with the financial resources they possessed and did not subscribe to the IPO plan.

TABLE 3.6

Response towards Demutualization of Regional Exchanges

(N=105)

Sr. No.	*Particular*	*Response*	*Number*	*Per centage*
1.	Favour Demutualization	Yes	43	41
2.	Favour Demutualization	No	62	59

The primary survey reveals that only minority of brokers (forty-one per cent) favour demutualization and majority of then (fifty-nine per cent) were against it. The brokers who were against demutualization felt that the regional exchanges would go out of their control and their role into the functioning of these regional exchanges would be reduced. The management of these exchanges would pass on to professional competent board who would work for the benefit and growth of the regional exchange rather than looking into the interest of only the broking community.

The minority felt that there was strong need to segregate ownership from management so that more experts can be inducted on the board to revamp the functioning of these exchanges which were till now operating for looking into the interest of big brokers as they had control on the composition of the board till now. With demutualization their role would be limited and professional board would be able to guide the growth of the regional exchange to enhance investor confidence and attract one of the best corporate practices by sharing the experiences and knowledge. Since experts from diverse background, knowledge and experience shall be inducted on the board which would enhance the process of revival or diversification of the regional exchanges.

3.4 DIVESTMENT OF THE STAKE OF THE DEMUTUALISED/CORPORATISED EXCHANGE

The respondent per centage of seventy-six offered their willingness to relinquish their shareholding in favour of foreign investors to achieve the objective of revival and develop sustainable business model for these regional exchanges. (Table 3.7)

The respondents in such large number felt that post demutualization the exchanges would become independent profit making entities and would require to increase upon their capital and funds for furthering their growth and diversification activities. They further felt that the exchanges may also witness tie-ups or may divest a part of their capital to other national and international exchanges in order to fight global competition and this could help them in preparing for global competition.

However, a small per centage (23.81 per cent) of the respondents opposed the idea of divesting the stake of regional exchanges. These respondents felt that this strategy could lead to lose of control of these exchanges eventually in favour of bigger exchanges or international exchanges. They also feared increased volatility levels on account of suck stake divestment. Lastly, they opined that this step would be against the interests of large number of small regional investors as the regional exchanges through divestment would fall into laps of bigger institutions and play in hands of bigger national or international players.

TABLE 3.7

Response towards Divestment in Stake of Regional Exchanges

(N=105)

Sr. No.	*Response*	*Number*	*Per centage*
1.	Yes	80	76.19
2.	No	25	23.81

3.5 FACTOR ANALYSIS

Factor analysis was undertaken to study the factors related to governance of RSEs which play important role in revival of the regional exchanges. Various factors were considered according to the views of the experts which included the stock exchange officials, brokers and professionals. However, factors like ineffective regulation of stock exchange members or brokers, ineffective regulation of listed companies, unequal access to corporate announcements and non-performance of outside independent directors were the most prominent as cited by experts.

Table 3.8 reveals that the respondents have given highest factor loading of .753 to non-performance of outside independent directors. The lowest factor loading of .525 is given to unequal access to corporate announcements. Other factors like ineffective regulation of listed companies (.687) and ineffective regulation of stock exchange members or brokers (.649) are also the other factors which have been accorded high factor loading.

Majority of the respondents have felt that the outside directors on the board of these RSEs have made insignificant or almost minimal contribution towards governance of these exchanges. The directors which were public nominees or nominees on board of such exchanges by Ministry of Finance and SEBI were not having adequate knowledge themselves or

TABLE 3.8

Analysis of Total Factors

Sr. No.	*Name and Factor*	*Constituent*	*Factor Loading*
Factor I	Growth-oriented	Low Regional Market Size	.589
		Few Listing	.586
		Limited free float	.559
		Stagnation in No. of Shareholders	.627
		Inadequate growth of unit holders	.440
		Statutory minimal share ownership	.607
		Lack of market Education	.801
		Lack of broad investors	.701
Factor II	Governance	Ineffective regulation of members	.649
		Ineffective regulation of Listed Co.	.687
		Unequal access to corporate announcements	.525
		Non-performance of outside directors	.753
Factor III	Economic Factors	Division of Liquidity and Distortion of price discovery	.751
		Cost Inefficiency For All Stakeholders	.749
		Complexities In Operations	.757
		Lack of Inter-Exchange Competition	.786
		Limited Revenue	.649
		Inequitable Burden Sharing	.574
		Low Level of Capital Expenditure	.559
		No Financial Guarantee	.602
		Low levels of actual settlement	.559
		Concentation of Liquidity and Market Capitalisation	.627
		Dominance of Badla financing	.753
		Excessive volatility	.607
Factor IV	Investor Protection	Inadequate investor protection	.602
Factor V	Working System	Few Professional	.567
		Lack of training and development	.579
		Inability to develop new products	.634
		Weak Criteria to become a member/ broker/market maker	.601
		Barrier to entry of new intermediaries	.654
		Membership card treated as investment instrument	.751
		Low capitalization of brokers	.621

experience in governance of the stock exchanges or had little knowledge about operations of capital markets and thus they were guided by the interests of the broker directors, who were busy in looking after their own interests rather than better governance of the stock exchanges. This was followed by ineffective regulation of listed companies and ineffective regulation of stock brokers who had politicized the boards and governance of these RSEs which had subsequently created an atmosphere where professionals and educated persons shrieked from coming forward and joining the board. These conditions deteriorated the governance of the RSEs and almost no or inadequate accountability and improper governance prevailed over the RSEs.

This has made a serious impact on the revival of these exchanges. The broker directors were always guided by their own interest and hence were always divided into political groups to led down each other rather than seriously think about or study about the revival of these exchanges. The independent directors could neither contribute on the revival as they were hardly having any knowledge or expertise in capital markets or stock exchanges.

Inadequate Investor Protection

Factor analysis was also conducted to understand the adequacy of investor protection carried out by the regional exchanges. A factor loading of .602 is observed. The respondents feel that the capital markets in the country provided for inadequate investor protection which is observed from a high factor loading as above. The respondents feel that investors trading at RSEs did not had enough protection and were taken to ride by many listed companies on these RSEs. With little transparency and trading rules the investors had no mechanism of grievance redressal as they were at the mercy of the brokers who were also the owners of these RSEs. The brokers on these exchanges were not working for the interest of the small investor and were not transparent in their deals with such small investor.

The board of these exchanges constituted of brokers with few public nominees who were most of the time dysfunctional or had no interest in the issues of these exchanges which further eroded the investor confidence on these RSEs.

Working System

Further, factor analysis was undertaken to study and analyze the factors which effect the working of the RSEs. This analysis is important to understand the restructuring or reorganizing of the regional exchanges. The various factors responsible for effective and efficient working of the exchanges were discussed with the experts including the stock exchange officials, professionals and brokers. The following factors according to the experts which were most prominent like availability of few experts or professionals, lack of training and development, inability to develop new financial trading products, weak criteria to become a member broker or market maker, barrier to entry of new intermediaries, membership card treated as investment instrument and low capitalization or capital base of brokers were considered for this study.

The respondents in this study have cited few important factors like availability of few professionals and experts, lack of training and development, inability to develop new trading products, weak criteria to become a member broker or market maker, barrier to entry of new intermediaries, membership card treated as investment instrument, low capitalization of brokers with factor loading of .567, .579, .634, .601, .654, .751 and .621 respectively.

Highest factor loading of .751 is observed where membership card has been treated as investment instrument. The total number of brokers who are actively trading in regional stock exchanges have been less than the total membership. Most of the people who became members of these exchanges held these membership card as investment instruments just to sell them later on for considerable capital gains or appreciation and not for the purpose of operating their membership. Thus these memberships were defunct and not functional. These members were hardly interested in the RSEs and seldom participated in any activity of the exchange. The real purpose was to sell their membership to make capital gains and not to trade on these exchanges. Thus these members did not at all contribute to the working system of the exchanges and thus the working and related governance was only left to those broker members who were actively engaged in carrying out trading activity.

Least factor loading of .567 is observed in too few professionals. The respondents feel that presence of only few professionals as member brokers did not hamper the working system or contributed towards the betterment of the RSEs. Many of these professionals were not interested in contributing towards the working of the stock exchanges as they did not feel to be a part of the board which was much dominated by the politics of the regional stock exchanges and were averse to contribute towards the working systems of the RSEs.

High factor loading is also observed in other factors like barriers to entry of new intermediaries, inability to develop new products and weak criteria to become a member broker. The regional stock exchanges also suffered adversely because of strict guidelines of SEBI facilitating the entry of new intermediaries which did not match the sufficient criteria for becoming the intermediary. Further, these exchanges also were not able to develop new products and there was a weak criteria of becoming a member broker where a matriculate could become a broker without having any or sufficient background or knowledge of capital markets or stock markets.

3.6 ALTERNATIVE MODELS OF FUTURE STOCK EXCHANGES

Recent developments in financial markets have shattered the view that stock exchanges engage only in the listing and trading of securities, and related business lines, within their domestic economies. These changes indicate that over the next five years, three distinct business models: the Global Exchange, the Regional Exchange and the Diversified Exchange are likely to emerge in the stock exchange industry. Rather than a hierarchy of exchanges, the new structure will be an interlocking lattice with each exchange filling a distinct economic space and thriving on its specialties. Exchanges that fall outside of this framework may see their businesses falter in the face of exceptionally strong international competition.

Implications of the new business models for both the exchanges themselves and market users are far and wide. Stock exchange alliances, electronic trading, changes in the financial regulation and the changing importance of location are considered here. While the analysis is not exhaustive, it highlights the importance of considering what these changes mean to the operation of financial markets. It is expected that the discussion will lead to suggestions for strategic planning. Several trends will hasten the developments outlined here, including the role of technology, the behaviour of nation-state regulatory agencies, exchange demutualization, and the measurements of stock exchange success.

Changes in the Stock Exchange Industry

The stock exchange industry across the world is undergoing a change. From the clubby and open-outcry trading floors of fifteen years ago, nearly all exchanges have moved to electronic order-based regimes. Stock exchange alliances and agreements with non-exchange electronic trading facilities are appearing on a regular basis. Stock exchange regulation have been converging worldwide to a greater degree than at any previous time, presenting exchanges with both increased international exposure and competition. Value chains are also reorganizing as stock exchanges seek to maintain and increase revenues from traditional and new business activities. As the current evolution matures, a new structure for global financial markets is expected to take a concrete shape. This framework will have a significant ramifications for both the financial markets worldwide and the users of these markets.

The use of technology is likely to infuse fundamental shifts and may alter the entire financial market landscape. Technology is also a major tool for cross border exchange alliances, since exchanges with compatible trading systems will be able to begin joint operations much faster than their counterparts. The extensive use of technology may also remove the human element from the exchange activities, with potentially damaging effects in infrastructure development and market surveillance. Not only does the manager of trading at an exchange have options for systems; now market users, including investors, intermediaries and issuers, may choose from several exchanges and even non-exchange facilities, based on their personal interests.

The fabric of stock exchanges is tightly interwoven with the identity of its nation-state. Exchanges are regulated according to the financial jurisdictions that are most often bounded by nation-states and provincial governments, and national or provincial regulations can significantly support or hinder stock exchange activities. Regulatory decisions to stimulate capital markets, in particular, may result in more domestic competition for security trading. While the convergence of regulations among several financial jurisdictions may present exchanges with greater opportunities to integrate into other national markets, it may give rise to numerous threats from abroad.

For stock exchanges, the financial success of the enterprises itself has assumed importance in recent years. Exchanges, in fact, are small and medium size businesses like many others, albeit subject to intense regulations by government authorities. They seek out economic roles in the marketplace, form short-term and permanent alliances and suffer from competition. Out of the 52 member exchanges of the FIBV, Australian stock exchange is now publicly and commercially held accountable; Stockholm is a wholly owned subsidiary of another company, while several others including New York, NASDAQ, Hong Kong, Singapore, Toronto, and Paris are exploring their options, and are demutualized Exchanges.

With these developments, success will be reflected in both the corporate profits of the bourse and the ability of an exchange to channel knowledge of its listed companies to interested investors. Other benchmarks for success such as the bid-ask spread, may continue to be useful as performance measures, though other indicators in the context of global competition are yet to emerge. Additional information that is crucial in this process pertains to the number of private and institutional investors, the capital inflows in the market by geographic origination that requires extensive IT participation from the community of financial intermediaries, some level of knowledge base in local and international industries and diversification of information dissemination. However, the three business models discussed here are not organized in a hierarchical pattern.

3.6.1 The Global Exchange (GEX)

The Global Exchange (GEX) would be a prototype of large exchange of today. It may be New York Stock Exchange or a London Stock Exchange, or what may be any one of several physical or virtual stock exchange alliances. It is the exchange with the highest total market capitalization in its region where companies outside the immediate jurisdictional radius of the GEX come for the high profile listing that enjoys extensively both in terms of cost of capital and in marketing its financial and commercial presence more broadly. One way to characterize the GEX is to demarcate zones of influence, larger than international commercial trade agreements and more attuned to the direction of capital flows, by trading partners or by the relationship between economic capitals and their related regions.

Operation of GEX

The Global Exchange dominates an economically linked community of several financial jurisdictions. It has the largest market capitalization in that community and the greatest trading volume and liquidity of any of its direct competitors. It trades both highly visible international securities and derivative products, whether as global shares, local currency depository receipts, or secondary listings of shares whose home market is elsewhere, as well as local shares from its own well developed domestic market. It draws its clientele from a pool of both domestic and global investors.

The first most important issue is understanding "an economically linked community". It can be NAFTA, the European Union, SAARC, BRIC or ASEAN and so on. What can be robustly stated is that in terms of globalization, the nation-state is obsolete as a default indicator for where a company will list. More important are questions of marketing, market visibility and the ease of capital raising which will all be determined by the broad economic community of the company.

The next issue is liquidity. In this context, liquidity means the ease with which investors can facilitate a trade and the cost they incur purchasing and disposing of securities and derivative products. Liquidity is contingent upon orders of instruments. The more orders flow in an exchange for a given instrument, the greater the liquidity. While liquidity is the ultimate product of an organized financial market, it is in itself the sum of a series of disparate factors.

Finally, what are highly visible international securities and derivatives products versus a local share in a national market? International securities may be from multinational companies, initially based in the home market or abroad. By contrast, a local national stock is a listed company known primarily within the bounds of a nation-state or market jurisdiction. A local security from the same financial jurisdiction as a GEX may be listed on that GEX, though local national stocks from other jurisdictions would tend to seek another home, as they would likely get lost in this larger market.

While in USA, the New York Stock Exchange appears to dominate as a GEX with the NASDAQ perhaps not far behind, in other regions the issue is of less consequence. In Europe, a GEX may be an independent London Stock Exchange, a London-Deutsche Bourse alliance, or a broader based pan-European alliance with London at its center. In Asia, potential GEX are Tokyo and Hong Kong-Shanghai. Regardless of the current economic condition of its nation-state, Tokyo is the capital of Asia's largest economy. A Hong Kong-Shanghai alliance, in a well-managed greater Chinese economy, would have tremendous potential.

Several other exchanges currently not considered as major contenders may attempt to gain GEX status. These include Singapore for a Pan-Southeast Asian Exchange, an international alliance of NASDAQ affiliates and Madrid for a cross Latin American-European Exchange. Another possibility is an exchange that currently exists only on paper; the International Securities Exchange. These are all "what if" possibilities. However, the right combination of factors such as economic, political, legislative, fiscal, technological, and sociological can make it happen much faster than anyone can guess.

The potential of coalition exchanges, whether virtual or with a physical presence, is tremendous. By pooling their resources, several smaller national exchanges can create centers of liquidity to compete with GEX, especially if they are able to merge duplicate listings of securities, combine their infrastructures and attract more market users than the aggregate of the exchanges individually. The possibilities of a coalition-based GEX increase as the technology makes trading a matter of observing one screen for many markets, or when enough exchanges using compatible technology decide to merge in a future era of demutualized exchanges.

At the surface level, the GEX appears to be in a comfortable position and benefits will accrue in the form of revenues from the trading of highly demanded securities and listing revenues from both international blue chips and national securities. The GEX will gain significant income from channeling the financial information flow for the world's leading businesses. The GEX is also expected to enjoy a certain prestige with international financial institutions and with the general public. However, GEX will face real competition from both other exchanges and non-exchange trading facilities. Since competitors tend to focus on the leader and rally around the chance to carve out a market share at its expense.

3.6.2 The Regional Exchange (REX)

The Regional Exchange (REX) is an exchange that concentrates on its region or nation-state. It has assumed this position either by choice or on account of circumstances. The most successful REX will always be conscious of its role and try to seek maximum revenue by way of expertise in its regional markets. In contrast to the GEX, the REX does not seek to be all things to all direct and indirect market users, including investors, issuers and intermediaries wherever they may be. It has selected its region, products and markets and promotes only its specialties.

Operation of REX

The Regional Exchange dominates in the local economy. It has the highest concentration of regional listings available and is the chief expert in these listings. By virtue of its intense national concentration, its index becomes a barometer of the health of the publicly quoted part of the regional economy. It may trade securities, commodities, derivative and other products. It draws its clientele primarily from regional investors with a smaller share of international investors interested in benefiting from the available expertise and opportunities.

The word region refers to a geographic area most often recognized as the nation-state, though not unique to it. In the event that the nation-state is an economically small entity, one REX may be the dominant player for the entire nation. When the nation-state is large, the REX may be the economic center for only a part of the region or state. Amsterdam is a good example of a REX at the national level, while a regional Spanish exchange such as the Bolsa de Bilbao is more of a specialist market.

Analogous to the GEX, the chief revenue sources of the REX are the listing and trading of national securities and the channeling of knowledge on the securities on its market. With the exception of some blue chips that may have an additional listing on a GEX, the REX will be the location with the highest liquidity for trading its national or niche stocks, bonds, futures, options, commodities and other financial products. The REX will offer many of the products that are evident today in national exchanges: index creation and monitoring, dissemination of share prices and the listing of domestic securities.

The REX will retain a strategic asset in the channeling of financial knowledge that is disseminated locally and internationally, both by virtue of its liquidity and its geographic and social proximity to listed companies. For expanding its business activities, the REX might choose to offer its promotional services to local firms. Accessing a multi-exchange screen system, a REX might project, for a fee, the latest announcements of a firm to pre-selected investor screens across the world. The value-added for the exchange, therefore, lies in the technology, the channeling of information, and most importantly, the ability to segment its market users.

Among others, the exchanges in Copenhagen, Oslo, Helsinki and Tel Aviv have already begun this type of marketing activity. In one form or the other, they disseminate company information to interested brokers, institutional and retail investors that the exchange itself is required by law to receive. In Copenhagen, distribution is currently by fax; online and email access will begin soon. In Oslo, a subsidiary, Oslo Børs Information A.F., has been established for this purpose. No content analysis is provided. Competition is light, although companies such as Reuters may soon present more of a challenge in other corners of the world. Even so, exchanges are legally required to receive information of material importance to the financial value of listed enterprises, and so they benefit from a competitive advantage.

As with projecting information over a screen, the real value in this service will be the ability of an exchange to segment the market and provide specific pieces of information to pre-selected clients. Currently, data marketing companies around the world use their skills in segmentation to reap profits for themselves and their clients. In the age of demutualization and with the information value chain undergoing reorganization, there is no reason to believe that stock exchanges cannot do it. Exchanges can successfully apply the market segmentation principle to reformulating historical information releases or quotes in one security from several facilities where a security is traded in accordance with the needs of individual investors. A by-product of a successful information-delivery service will be that the exchanges are seen as authoritative centers of knowledge related to their business of listing and trading shares. With a growing reputation as a reliable source of refined information and not just raw data, exchanges should see significant revenues from this business.

In trading, Regional Exchanges may also develop national niches, such as Stockholm and Helsinki in mobile telecommunications and Oslo in shipping. These niches will merge naturally with the strength of the local economy, and listing and trading in niche sectors will increase at the specialty bourses. International investors will be drawn to niche exchanges because of the increased liquidity for sector securities, and for the human infrastructure in sector knowledge, legal frameworks and trading patterns that begets this liquidity. Indices will be developed to track niche sector securities by geographic region or worldwide. Securities market niches may also be developed outside of particular industries, such as for Employee Stock Option Plans (ESOPs), and will keep users tied to markets for the same infrastructure reasons as noted above. Both exchanges with niches and those without will likely trade a combination of national blue chip stocks that are listed and traded on several other exchanges, and a large number of mid-cap securities that are listed and traded only at the REX or on very few other markets.

The REX must educate its nation-state or regional economic development agencies as to the nature of the exchange industry and what exchanges bring to wealth creation.

It can be also argued that domestic investors will invest in local stocks over GEX stocks because they are more comfortable with them; familiarity breeds local expertise, and this is compounded when the same investors see the brand names in the store and in their media on a daily basis. This in theory will keep local investors from fleeing the REX altogether and may result in a stronger sense of national pride in the REX. The REX can capitalize on this by showcasing its well performing national securities to domestic investors. Assuming also that more capital flows to the GEX, over time the multiples become more attractive at a REX than at a GEX and capital flows back.

The existence of the REX is vital for the functioning of global capital markets, of which the REX is the local representative and facilitator. As with a GEX, the most difficult challenge for an exchange is recognizing that its strengths lie as a REX and developing a business strategy that capitalizes on this understanding.

3.6.3 The Diversified Exchange (DEX)

The Diversified Exchange (DEX) is similar to the Regional Exchange, except that it enjoys not only the listing and trading of national securities but also has a core competency in at least one more related business line. This type of exchange has recognized that it has a strong economic purpose beyond its role in the issuing and trading business; it is a hybrid enterprise. In this aspect, the DEX may compete globally in a variety of fields like any other business. The DEX is not limiting itself to the traditional role in the marketplace, and has therefore, significant ramifications for the exchange industry in an age of increasing competition.

Operation of a Diversified Exchange

The Diversified Exchange primarily operates in the regional economy but also engages in economic activities outside the usual sphere reserved for exchanges. It has the greatest concentration of regional listings available and is the chief expert in these listings. It may trade securities, derivative products, or both. It draws its clientele primarily from regional investors with a smaller share of international investors. In its other activities, it competes with firms that are totally distinct from GEX or REX in economic form and function.

Three examples of DEX exist today: one with a technology focus, a second with an economic development focus and a third that is a division of a broader company. All three are distinct business models and show that the success of a DEX is not fixed in one broad direction, unlike that of a GEX and a REX. These hybrid exchanges may focus on particular business lines or geographical expansion, though all are focused on making profits and identifying new opportunities for growth.

In the sphere of technology, exchanges that sell software outside the exchange industry environment face a huge and competitive market. Available evidence indicates that marketable products generally arise from the in-house development of new technologies. The development of its system capitalized on a long-term engagement with computation and technology. From its trading activity development, Paris formed a subsidiary, Groupe GL, to allow trader access to multiple stock exchanges from one computer screen. Groupe GL is now one of the market leaders in this field worldwide and in 1998 accounted for 32% of revenues of Groupe SBF-Paris Bourse's consolidated accounts.

In economic development, the bourses in Johannesburg and Istanbul diversified into this field out of the necessity of helping develop neighbour market economies to strengthen their own domestic socioeconomic environment. While some of this work is self-serving, it also shows that an exchange can be an active regional player, both for mutual success and for profit. Currently, the Johannesburg Stock Exchange has offered its proprietary trading system to all the neighboring countries of southern Africa. In another 20 years, this might result in a technologically unified Southern African exchange that will be recognized as a large REX, whereas now South Africa alone is seen as a small but highly developed market by the international investment community. Whether the Johannesburg Stock Exchange is the driver of this unification or the Southern African Development Community takes the lead, the Johannesburg bourse will obviously play a major role. Istanbul's role in the Federation of Euro-Asian Stock Exchanges has been similar to that of Johannesburg in the Balkan region and in the Turkic-speaking countries lying to the east.

Exchanges themselves may now be bought and absorbed by a non-exchange business if market conditions were right, or created by a partnership between an exchange and a non-exchange business.

The DEX may not seem to exist as a category. Fundamentally, however, these exchanges are operating as parts of business concerns outside the arena of listing, trading and channeling information of securities. This puts them in a different business model that GEX and REX.

3.7 CONCLUSION

The study concludes that revival of regional exchanges can be achieved through both diversification and reorganizing or restructuring strategies. The diversification strategy may include revival of the regional exchanges by adding new businesses into its portfolio which may include portfolio management, commodities trading, marketing of investment products, merchant/investment banking, dematerializing facilities, operating as representative trading centers for the national exchanges and offering foreign exchange/SME trading platform.

The re-organizing of these RSEs may involve revival of the RSEs through any or combination of these, firstly revival through restructuring of the RSEs by demutualization of these exchanges secondly allowing for the divestment of the stake of the demutualised/corporatised exchange, thirdly by allowing the regional exchanges to form a single consolidated entity to compete with the other two bigger exchanges like NSE and BSE and fourthly providing exit route for the RSEs which desire withdrawal of recognition.

Further factor analysis reveals that the respondents have given highest factor loading of .753 to non-performance of outside independent directors on the board of the regional exchanges and lowest factor loading of .525 is given to unequal access to corporate announcements.

Factor analysis also concluded that the adequacy of investor protection carried out by the regional exchanges bore a factor loading of .602. The respondents feel that the capital markets in the country provided for inadequate investor protection which is observed from a high factor loading as above. The respondents feel that investors trading at RSEs did not had enough protection and were taken to ride by many listed companies on these RSEs.

The respondents in this study have concluded that important factors like availability of few professionals and experts, lack of training and development, inability to develop new trading products, weak criteria to become a member broker or market maker, barrier to entry of new intermediaries, membership card treated as investment instrument and so on are some of the prominent reasons or factors which have adversely affected the working of the regional exchanges.

New developments in the basic business of stock exchanges have shattered the traditional view that exchanges engage only in the listing and trading of securities within their domestic economies. In the near future, the stock exchange industry will see the emergence of three distinct business models: the Global Exchange, the Regional Exchange and the Diversified Exchange. Exchanges that fall outside of these business models may see their businesses falter in the face of stringent international competition.

The business models outlined in this study share one significant feature outside the listing and trading of securities: each of these fill a distinct economic space and thrive on respective specialities. Although competition with other exchanges and from non-exchange trading facilities cannot be ruled out, exchanges of all categories can prosper in global and moderately healthy economy. The key to success is the ability to identify strengths in infrastructure and expertise, develop cooperative relationships with government regulators and effectively promote selected business lines, based on existing strategic advantages. A diverse lattice of strong capital market institutions is to the benefit of both market users and operators.

Notes and References

1. Johnson and Scholes (2006), "Exploring Corporate Strategy: Text and Cases, Prentice Hall; 7th edition.
2. Hax, A.C and Majluf, N.S. (1996), The Strategy Concept and Process, A Pragmatic Approach, Upper Saddle River, NJ, Prentice Hall.
3. Porter, M.E. (1985), Competitive Advantage: creating and sustaining superior performance. New York: The Free Press

CONCLUSIONS AND SUGGESTIONS

In this chapter, the main findings of the study and the suggestions stemming therefrom are enumerated. For the sake of brevity, conclusions and suggestions are presented separately, in order to meet the objectives of the study both secondary and primary data was collected and have been used as part of analysis.

4.1 NEED FOR REVIVAL

For about 20 years regional stock exchanges created wealth for the society that was decimated in one go. The regional stock exchanges started experiencing a decline as early as 1996-97 with the inception of fully computerized NSE. While the BSE was quick to take a cue from it and started online trading, the other RSEs lagged behind. By the time they woke up and decided to computerise, it was too late. The two national stock exchanges had already usurped their markets with their wide reach. More and more companies began listing at the national stock exchanges. Investors too preferred online trading. The majority of the 19 regional stock exchanges (RSEs) experienced minimal or nil trading. Dozens of companies delisted from these exchanges to seek place at the National Stock Exchange (NSE) and the Bombay Stock Exchange (BSE); their online trading and professional management made them the favourite of investors and companies alike.

Nearly all the RSEs had to take the subsidiary route to ensure their members' survival. However, for the stock exchanges themselves, there was no reprieve. Their trading infrastructure, worth crores of rupees, continues to be idle.

The management of these RSEs deep down, feel the need for a radical change to revive the exchanges. Some of them consider the merger of all RSEs into one entity as the only long-term solution. But till that time, they have pinned their hopes on Indonext. The Federation of stock exchanges and various RSEs have chalked out a plan to revive the regional stock exchanges. They have proposed to create Indonext, a single order book, for trading by all RSEs. This will provide an impetus to all inactive RSEs and put them on the path to revival by diversifying their business model, the RSEs can look forward for revival. In USA, there are around 55 different stock exchanges. At present, there exist 19 regional stock exchanges in India. In future, every exchange will have a distinct identity of its own. For instance, NASDAQ in US is well known in so far as the technology companies are concerned. Similarly, AIM at London attracts SMEs from all over the world. RSEs should study the pattern of transactions in order to create a niche for them. Their salvation is possible.

4.2 OBJECTIVES

The main objective of the present study is to examine the present position of the regional stock exchanges in the country and to suggest strategies for their revival. To achieve this main objective following secondary objectives have been identified which are listed as below:

1. To examine the growth and current status or position of the Regional Stock Exchanges (RSEs) in the country.

2. To study the scope for diversification of the functions of RSEs.
3. To find out the possibility of Re-organizing the RSEs.
4. To assess the role of RSEs in managing the problem of non-liquid as well as thinly traded or non-traded stocks.
5. To suggest a business model for revival to ensure viability of RSEs.

4.3 MAJOR FINDINGS

1. The primary survey revealed that 85 out 105 (81 per cent) respondents replied in the affirmative that regional stock exchanges have lived up to their expectations while remaining 20 (19 per cent) replied in the negative. They further opined that easy physical reach to investors and brokers, financial strength, physical infrastructure, managerial expertise, meeting aspirations of small regional investor and regional capital formation as the strengths of the regional exchanges.
2. All the respondents were of the opinion that they had an easy physical access to the regional exchanges to pursue their investment objectives and this facilitated the trading and primary market activities on account of nearness to the broking facilities.
3. Twenty-seven per cent of the respondents felt that the regional capital formation has received a jolt with lesser number of companies now coming out with public issues. Moreover, the regional companies which were being traded on these exchanges got themselves delisted after doing away of mandatory listing by SEBI. This further aggravated the situation since the regional exchanges lost their business and earnings in the form of listing fee, on one hand, and the regional investor was hit the hardest, on the other hand, in the form of increase in the non-traded shares as a

result of delisting. He could not sell or buy anymore these shares and thus lost heavily the capital invested in such scrips or companies.

4. Over half of the respondents (51.7 per cent) were of the opinion that the regional stock exchanges had adequate infrastructure to support its ongoing as well as future activities. As stated earlier the new and latest infrastructure which has been created is sufficient to meet the growing needs of the brokers, exchange administration and investors.
5. Sixty per cent of the respondents replied that the exchange was providing services to the investors due to its financial strength and this helped the exchange to create and strengthen new infrastructure as per its need. The financial strength of these exchanges facilitated purchase of new land and more space with modern building architecture that provides space to all the brokers, administrative staff and officers of the exchange and in some cases the excess space created has even been leased out on rentals to banks and insurance companies.
6. The survey revealed that thirty seven per cent of the respondents felt that the regional stock exchanges had played an important role in meeting the aspirations of the regional investors. They felt more confident in investing in regional companies as they could trace the history of promoters, quality of management and the nature of industry. Such information enabled them to take suitable decisions regarding investment in these companies. The regional investor was provided with unique handsome opportunity to gain by way of these investment avenues and was happy to invest through regional exchanges.
7. Thirty-eight per cent of the respondents opined that the managerial and technical expertise in these exchanges met the expectations of the investors but this area requires further

improvement. Managerial and technical expertise is an important strength for any enterprise to survive and sustain in long-run. Adequate number of professionals (with finance, legal and investment background) is required to manage these exchanges since experts are in a better position to understand the dynamics and act accordingly.

8. The survey revealed that 19 per cent of the respondents felt that regional stock exchanges have not lived up to their expectations and they listed the weaknesses of the regional exchanges as limited number of companies or lack of liquidity for trading, non-transparent and inefficient trading and clearing mechanism, poor quality of governance board, inappropriate technology and non-resolution of investor grievances.
9. Forty-five per cent of the respondents opined that the regional stock exchanges had not provided an efficient and transparent trading and clearing mechanism for the settlement of their trades until computerized trading and a uniform settlement was introduced by the market regulator. The brokers in RSEs were always looked with suspicion by the investors' as to the rate of a particular deal being executed by the broker on his behalf, because the investor had no access to know the correctness of the price of the deal as he was not allowed any access to the trading hall of the stock exchange.
10. The study finds that eighty-five per cent of the respondents out of those who felt that regional exchanges have not lived up to their expectations replied that the regional stock exchange lacked liquidity. By liquidity they meant they had limited choice to trade in a large number of listed and permitted securities. This is one prime reason for the investors' alienation from the regional stock exchanges and shifting their business towards the national exchanges.

11. Thirty-five per cent of the respondents opined that due to poor quality of governance of the board of these regional exchanges, they were unable to sustain their business or growth. The board of directors constituted at the regional exchanges were always guided by the interest of the broking community or their political groups which guided the interest of the exchange to meet their own interest rather than the interest of all the stake holders. This was also stated as one of the main reason for demutualization or corporatisation of the regional exchanges so that their governance may pass on to more professional and independent directors who are experts from different financial areas. This was necessary to bring in transparency in the functioning of these exchanges.
12. Thirty-five per cent of the respondents were of the opinion that the regional exchanges were facing lack of technology up-gradation or possessed obsolete technology and were not fit for conducting trading operations. The regional exchanges had made no investment or minimal investment in technology up-gradation and were following the outdated, outcry, method of trading with a centralized trading ring. There was manual system of record keeping and settlement process was slow and inefficient, which led to delay in receiving payments by the investors who had sold their scrips, or receiving shares by the investors who had bought the shares. The actual period of receiving payment was as long as 30 to 35 days.
13. Twenty per cent of the respondents were critical of the non-resolution of investors' grievances and felt that the respective regional stock exchanges had inadequate grievance redressal mechanism or lacked transparent functioning. The credentials of the brokers and the respective exchanges were doubtful.
14. Government's Policy and role of SEBI with a

weighted average mean score of 15.33 has been ranked at number 1 position as the most prominent factor responsible for fall of business of regional exchanges by the respondents. They are of the opinion that the government's policies related to functioning of the capital markets, and in particular, the secondary market or stock exchanges, were aimed at highest sense of investor protection. This shift in the government's attitude provided a larger role for the market regulator to achieve this objective. The regulator, thus, in the larger interest of the population moved to provide equal opportunity to the investors throughout the length and breadth of the nation by introducing real time access to trades through electronic trading, a transparent and uniform trading cycle across the country. The respondents opined that this policy found favour with the investors and they shifted their business interest from small regional exchanges to bigger exchanges like NSE and BSE. The brokers of regional exchanges thus lost their business to the bigger exchanges.

15. Growing problem of illiquid or thinly traded stocks with a weighted average mean score of 13.96 has been ranked at number 2 position as another prominent reason for fall in business of RSEs. The respondents felt that the liquidity blocked in illiquid or non-traded/thinly traded scrips have had a negative impact on the business of the regional exchanges. Many investors find their money blocked in these scrips which were once traded on these regional exchanges but are no more traded after their closure.
16. Preference of investor's towards bigger exchanges like NSE and BSE with a weighted average mean score of 12.71 has been ranked at number 3 position as a factor responsible for fall of business by the respondents. The respondents were of the view that the rise of the national stock exchange resulted in problem of liquidity for the regional

stock exchanges as more stocks were traded on the national exchanges and hence preference of the investing population to trade on the national exchange grew amongst the investors.

17. Quality of management of companies listed on regional exchanges with a weighted average mean score of 12.07 has been ranked at number 4 position as another factor responsible for fall in business of regional exchanges. The respondents felt that it was the poor quality of management of the companies listed on these exchanges which has resulted in fall of business of these exchanges. These companies defied providing adequate safety of capital and returns to the investors and instead, the promoters have benefited in person and made huge profits by manipulating and price rigging of the share price thus resulting in loss to the common investor.
18. Loss of investors' faith in the regional stock exchanges with a weighted average mean score of 11.93 has been ranked at number 5 position as a factor responsible for fall of their business. The respondents opined that the fall in business of regional stock exchanges is attributed to loss or lack of investor faith in functioning of these exchanges which were till now run by the broker community themselves with negligible or no role of independent professionals or directors. The regional stock exchanges according to them functioned by way of autocratic governance as their managing boards constituted largely the working brokers who were interested only, in looking after their own interest. The trading mechanism and settlements were governed by the brokers' community without any role of independent professionals or authorities.
19. General economic conditions prevailing in the economy with a weighted average mean score of 10.82 has been ranked at number 6 position by the respondents as yet another factor responsible for

fall in business of regional exchanges. The respondents felt that it was the lack of economic and industrial growth in the region which has led to fall in business of regional exchange.

20. Growing interest of investors' in primary market with a weighted average mean score of 10 has been ranked at number 7 position as one of the factors responsible for fall in the trading business of regional exchanges. The respondents felt that the shift of the investors' towards large sized IPOs has resulted in fall of business in secondary markets. The returns provided by these IPO's along with safety of capital was the reason responsible for this shift.
21. Lack of good governance practices in the regional exchanges with a weighted average mean score of 9.60 has been ranked at number 8 position by the respondents as another factor contributing towards fall in business of regional exchanges. The respondents felt that the business in the regional exchanges fell because of the lack of these good corporate governance practices. The brokers could not bring about professionalism in running of these exchanges and hence ruled over the much larger investor interest by overriding it with their own economic interest.
22. Lack of transparency in functioning of the regional exchanges with a weighted average mean score of 8.87 has been ranked at number 9 position by the respondents as the last factor responsible for fall in their business. The respondents have contributed the fall of business at the regional exchanges to lack of transparency in operations that has eroded the confidence of the investing population in the regional exchange. They also opined that malpractices like insider trading, delay in settlement period and non-redressal of investor complaint or grievance and so on are some of the reasons where investors' have lost faith in functioning of regional exchanges.

23. Poor composition of board or governance with a weighted average mean score of 17.89 has been ranked at number 1 position as the most prominent factor responsible for poor operating health of regional exchanges. While interacting with the respondents brokers it was opined that prior to demutualization of exchanges, the fellow brokers who were elected to the board of the regional exchanges were those who served the interest of the brokers group who got them elected. It was further pointed by the respondents that many of these brokers were neither having knowledge or foresight or expertise to lead the regional exchanges against dynamic changes happening in the capital markets. They were not prepared to take on the challenges posed by the NSE or BSE which were growing due to appropriate technology which helped them reach far off places and brought transparency into the trading mechanism thereby reposing increased investor confidence.
24. Structural changes in the financial markets with a weighted average mean score of 17.64 has been ranked at number 2 position as another important factor responsible for the downfall of the regional exchanges. The respondents further listed these structural changes as globalization of financial markets, introduction of screen-based online trading by NSE and BSE, uniform trading cycle, demutualization of exchanges, introduction of derivatives trading and introduction of depositories. They further opined that the reach of NSE to almost all corners of the country with screen-based trading virtually halted the businesses at the regional exchanges which could not match the technology and were not prepared to take on these challenges.
25. Problem of non-traded and thinly traded shares with a weighted average mean score of 16.21 has been ranked at number 3 position as another

reason for non-operativeness of the regional exchanges. The respondents further felt that growth in number of non-traded and thinly traded regional companies scrips' moved the investors interest from regional exchanges to bigger exchanges, where large number of scrips were available to trade. The trading activity was a direct source of revenue for the regional exchanges in form of turnover fees which was levied on all transactions conducted by the brokers of these exchanges. The shifting of trading interest to bigger exchanges and problem of non-traded or thinly traded shares has led to considerable fall in revenue and the regional exchanges have almost no source of revenue from trading activities as trading diminished from these exchanges to the bigger exchanges.

26. Lack of inter exchange competition opportunities amongst the regional exchanges on one hand and their competition with bigger exchanges with a weighted average mean score of 15.79 has been ranked at number 4 position as another factor that has led to closure of the smaller regional stock exchanges. The bigger exchanges have led from the front and have taken over almost all business activities from these exchanges making them unviable.
27. Decline or fall in listing fee which was one of the most important source of revenue for the regional exchanges with a weighted average mean score of 13.79 has been ranked at number 5 position as another factor responsible for making them non-operative. The respondents were further of the view that the decision of the regulator to provide option of delisting to the regional companies, led to substantial decrease of income of these exchanges. With most of the companies already not been actively traded and the others getting themselves delisted, these developments completed ruined the operating health of the regional exchanges.

28. Growing loss of faith of the investors in the systems and trading mechanism along with delayed settlement procedures with a weighted average mean score of 12.00 has been ranked at number 6 position as another prominent factor leading to downfall of the regional exchanges. The respondents further opined that the brokers of these regional exchanges who enjoyed a majority on the board, had lost faith and trust of the investors due to non-transparent trading mechanism and delayed settlement procedures adopted by the regional exchanges. The dominance of superior technology which was provided by the two bigger exchanges was a shot in the arm in this regard as the outcry system was replaced by the screen-based trading where the investor could sit in front of the screen and see the different trades and rates of shares of different companies on the screen and make decisions accordingly. This led to complete adoption of technology by the investors who had already deteriorated their faith and trust in brokers of regional exchanges. The business from the regional exchanges thus moved to bigger exchanges.
29. Inappropriate and poor technology available with the regional exchanges with a weighted average mean score of 11.68 has been ranked at number 7 position as yet another factor which led to poor operating health of the regional exchanges by the respondents. They further opined that the screen-based trading mechanism introduced by the bigger exchanges had far reach and coverage of the geographical area on one hand and also led to transparency in trading, thereby restoring or shifting investor interest from regional exchanges to bigger exchanges.
30. Factor analysis while studying the major factors related to growth and decline of regional exchanges observed that maximum factor loading of .801 is given to lack of market education and

minimum factor loading is in case of inadequate growth of unit holders. A large number of respondents feel that lack or inadequate market knowledge or education has been the main factor responsible for inadequate growth of RSEs. The investors operating in these regional stock exchanges have not had proper education upon the effect of globalization and integration of world capital markets and have thus lost considerable money and capital due to poor selection of stocks and have been unable to understand the market timings and trading strategies of FIIs *vis-a-vis* Indian Mutual Funds. These small investors have faced the burnt and have lost their considerable portion of invest able surplus in the bouts of technical rally and subsequent corrections that followed. In absence of adequate market education these investors were unable to sell or buy equities in these RSEs at the correct time and thus incurred huge losses and lost faith in the RSEs. However it is also revealed that factors like lack of broad investors (.701), stagnation in number of shareholders (.627) and statutory minimal share ownership (.607) are also some of the main factors which the respondents feel are important towards inadequate growth of RSEs.

31. The primary survey revealed that forty one per cent of the respondents were positive about the role of regional stock exchanges in the promotion of equity cult and the spread of the capital markets while the rest fifty-nine per cent of respondents opined that regional exchanges did not have much role in promoting the equity cult and spread of capital markets. The regional listing criteria was held to be main reason behind this. The mandatory regional listing on the regional exchange, on one hand, provided opportunities for the investors of the region to trade in that scrip but, on the other hand, restricted the opportunities for trading at national level or other exchanges.

32. The survey reveals that there are three major reasons for lack of liquidity on regional exchanges. First, the equity base of the listed stocks of a large number of companies was quite low. There are several companies with equity capital of less than Rs 3 crore due to historical reasons, such as low base of capital, public holding, etc. Second, the floating stock of listed securities, particularly those held by the public, is quite low. Third, there are no market-makers or specialists for non-traded or thinly traded shares, as in almost all the developed markets.
33. The survey reveals that factor analysis while analyzing the dominant factors that contribute towards the economic operations of the regional exchanges found that maximum factor loading of .786 is observed in lack of inter exchange competition, which according to them is a major factor contributing towards the poor economic health of these exchanges. The respondents feel that RSEs have not been able to provide enough opportunities for the investors as well the brokers to compete amongst each other. The mandatory regional listings of the companies on the regional stock exchange under whose ambit the company felt also was cited as one of the reason for distorting the inter exchange trading. Each of these regional exchange mostly traded in shares of its own listed companies and could not compete well with national exchange like NSE. This was a major cause for increase in number of illiquid/thinly traded or non-liquid shares, as regional listed companies provided constituted most of the trading opportunities for the regional investors. Further, once the regional stock exchanges were out of business, the regional companies had no platform to get their shares listed except for BSE or NSE but most of them were not able to meet the stringent listing criteria of these bigger exchanges and thus found no active trades.

Amongst the RSEs only BSE could survive as it was perceived as a national exchange before the emergence of NSE and maximum numbers of regionally listed companies were also traded on BSE. Least factor loading of .559 was observed in two factor namely low level of capital expenditure and low level of actual settlement. The respondents are of the opinion that low level of capital expenditure on infrastructure by the RSEs taken together with low level of actual settlement, i.e. most of the actual trades conducted on regional exchanges being speculative, the actual delivery of the stocks, was low.

34. The results of the data also reveal that the decline in the business of regional stock exchanges can be attributed to various reasons. The first and major is the establishment of National Stock exchange (NSE) in 1994 with an all India spread throughout the country and expansion of operations of Bombay stock Exchange (BSE), abolition of Badla with effect from July, 2001, introduction of uniform trading cycles at all the stock exchanges, introduction of rolling settlements from the year 2003 and shift of trading interest of RSE brokers to bigger exchanges due to absence of trading at the RSEs and finally withdrawing of the mandatory listing clause of regional companies as some of the other reasons responsible for decline in their business.
35. The survey results indicate that about sixty-seven per cent respondents were for the revival of the regional exchanges. The remaining thirty three per cent respondents opined that they are not in the favour of the revival of the exchange.
36. The survey reveals that seventy three per cent of the respondents were not aware of the revival solutions adopted by RSEs in other developed nations. Most of them were even ignorant about the status of the regional exchanges in other countries. The respondents were only aware about

the presence of major stock exchanges in the world. However, a small number (27 per cent) of the respondents were aware of the revival strategies or solutions related to RSEs in Europe and USA. They were aware about the Euro Next exchange which is conceived as a consolidated effort to bring together the regional exchanges of Europe. These respondents also favoured the concept of specialized exchanges, as in USA. The respondents also echoed some areas of concern related to revival of regional exchanges like adopting a sustainable business model, looking into regional aspirations of the investors' and entrepreneurs, identifying and diversifying into new areas of business and emerging as specialized exchanges of that region.

37. The survey reveals that majority (89.52 per cent) of the respondents were aware of the revival initiatives adopted by SEBI and only a few (10.48 per cent) were not aware of the same.
38. The survey reveals that out of the sixty seven per cent of the respondents who had favoured revival of the regional stock exchanges, opined that diversification and reorganization can be used as strategies to revive them. Seventy per cent of the respondents out of the above favoured the revival through the mode of diversification of businesses of these regional stock exchanges and thirty per cent were of the opinion that revival should be taken through the mode of reorganization of the regional stock exchanges.
39. The respondents when asked to rank the various activities which can be added in the existing business portfolio of the regional exchanges so as to revive them through diversification strategy ranked at number 1 position with a weighted average mean score of 13.22 introduction of portfolio management services as additional business activity and felt that the stock exchanges should diversify and provide this specialist service

to the investors of the region. The exchange can develop this service by recruiting specialists who are trained to carry such activities. The regional exchanges already have the required infrastructure including the hardware and software, specialist information on any scrip, library research and so on for managing such activity.

40. Commodities trading as a business option available to revive the regional exchanges with a weighted average mean score of 12.49 has been ranked at number 2 position by the respondents. The regional exchanges have already been given one time waiver to become member of both NCDEX and MCX via subsidiary route. The regional stock exchanges have already started providing the services of commodity trading to the investors in the region through their existing brokers. The regional exchanges have formed their subsidiary company to be member of these specialized exchanges and through its subsidiary the regional exchange is conducting all commodities related trading activities.
41. The survey reveals that Marketing of Investment Products as a lucrative business option available to revive the regional exchanges with a weighted average mean score of 10.73 ranked at number 3 position by the respondents. The regional stock exchanges have largest registered data base in terms of the investors in the region. These investors are clients to one or many brokers of these exchanges and further invest their savings into securities market with the advice of the brokers. The brokers influence a lot as opinion leaders for making investment. These brokers can generate lots of business for the exchange through their clients or investors by selling insurance, banking term deposits, mutual fund schemes and so on as to add to the business volume and returns of the regional stock exchange.
42. Merchant or Investment banking as a business

option which can be added to the portfolio of the regional exchanges with a weighted average mean score of 8.89 has been ranked at number 4 position by the respondents. The regional exchanges have all the necessary infrastructure required to carry on the activities of merchant banking. They can further recruit specialist professionals who can help or manage in carrying out these activities for the exchanges. In fact the regional stock exchanges can be one stop shops or partners for local entrepreneurs those to wish to tap the primary market and raise funds for their expansions, upcoming projects, diversification activities, etc. All what is required from the promoters is to file an application with the exchange and rest everything can be taken care of by the regional stock exchanges.

43. Opening of regional centers of bigger exchanges like NSE or BSE as addition into the present activities of the regional exchanges with a weighted average mean score of 8.87 has been ranked at number 5 position by the respondents. They further feel that the regional exchanges are open to charge fee from the bigger exchanges while extending services to investors, brokers and entrepreneurs in the region while representing the interest of these exchanges. The regional stock exchanges through their subsidiaries are already members of these two bigger exchanges. The regional exchanges can represent the interests of investor and entrepreneur of the region in which they are located by becoming centers of NSE or BSE.

44. Providing investor education and appropriate courses with a weighted average mean score of 8.56 has been ranked at number 6 position. The respondents feel that these courses can be for beginners level and also high end courses may be designed for building expertise into trading strategies. The need for investor education and

relevant courses has been felt more after the introduction of derivatives trading in India for which the investors have little knowledge and expertise as to how they can effectively make use of options and futures for minimizing their risk.

45. Providing dematerialization services with a weighted average mean score of 8.40 has been ranked at number 7 position by the respondents. They are of the opinion that the regional stock exchanges should become the depository participant with any of the two depositories or both and start demat services. This would not only help in generating income for the stock exchange but also facilitate the investor as these regional exchanges would become one-stop shops wherein apart from trading the investor can also open the demat account and enjoy these services under the same roof which shall be more convenient to him with respect to time and management of his account.

46. Operating as regional centre of SEBI with a weighted average mean score of 8.27 has been ranked at number 8 position as another business option available for the stock exchanges. The respondents were of this view as they felt that by doing this the investors' grievance and complaints redressal process shall get a boost as the investors shall only be needed to make a complaint to the official of SEBI who would be available all time at the regional exchange. This would hasten up the complaint redressal. At the same time the respondents felt that brokers and other intermediaries shall also effectively function as the presence of SEBI officials shall make them improve their functioning and the market regulator shall be able to effectively enlarge its vigil in the functioning of the capital markets, both primary and secondary by having its presence in these regional exchanges. A regional officer may be appointed by SEBI to head its presence in these regional exchanges.

47. The survey reveals that respondents with a weighted average mean score of 7.33 at number 9 position opined that the regional exchanges must diversify into forex trading and SME trading. They felt that it would provide business opportunity to the brokers of these exchanges on one hand and shall provide an opportunity to the regional small and medium entrepreneur to raise capital but also look into his foreign exchange requirement by ways of trading on these exchanges. The regional investor as well as the industry would be facilitated when the regional exchanges shall start providing these services.
48. The survey reveals that re-organizing of the RSEs may involve revival of the RSEs through any or combination of these, firstly revival through restructuring of the RSEs by demutualization of the regional exchanges secondly allowing for the divestment of the stake of the demutualised or corporatised exchange and thirdly providing exit route for the RSEs which desire withdrawal of recognition.
49. The survey finds that forty one per cent of the respondents of the regional exchanges were in the favour of demutualization and subsequently offering an IPO to the investing public to augment their financial resources for the growth of the business activities at the exchanges. The remaining fifty-nine per cent were not in favour of the demutualization scheme and were satisfied with the financial resources they possessed and did not subscribe to the IPO plan.
50. The survey reveals that seventy six per cent respondents favoured the opinion of relinquishing the present shareholding in favour of foreign investors to achieve the objective of revival and develop sustainable business model for these regional exchanges. The respondents in such large number felt that post demutualization the

exchanges would become independent profit making entities and would require to increase upon their capital and funds for furthering their growth and diversification activities. They further felt that the exchanges may also witness tie-ups or may divest a part of their capital to other national and international exchanges in order to fight global competition and this could help them in preparing for global competition.

51. A small per centage (23.81 per cent) of the respondents opposed the idea of divesting the stake of regional exchanges. These respondents felt that this strategy could lead to lose of control of these exchanges eventually in favour of bigger exchanges or international exchanges. They also feared increased volatility levels on account of suck stake divestment. Lastly they opined that this step would be against the interests' of large number of small regional investor as the regional exchanges through divestment would fall into laps of bigger institutions and play in hands of bigger national or international players.

52. The factor analysis conducted to study the dominant factors related to governance of the regional exchanges reveals that respondents have given highest factor loading of .753 to non-performance of outside independent directors as one of the reasons for poor governance of the regional exchnages. The lowest factor loading of .525 is given to unequal access to corporate announcements. Other factors like ineffective regulation of listed companies (.687) and ineffective regulation of stock exchange members or brokers (.649) are also the other factors which have been accorded high factor loading.

53. Factor analysis conducted to understand the adequacy of investor protection carried out by the regional exchanges found that a high factor loading of .602 is observed whereby the

respondents feel that the capital markets in the country provided for inadequate investor protection which is observed. The respondents opined that investors' trading at RSEs did not had enough protection and were taken to ride by many listed companies on these RSEs. With little transparency and trading rules the investors had no mechanism of grievance redressal as they were at the mercy of the brokers who were also the owners of these RSEs. The brokers on these exchanges were not working for the interest of the small investor and were not transparent in their deals with such small investor.

54. The factor analysis while studying the major factors affecting the working system of the regional exchanges reveals highest factor loading of .751 is observed in case of membership card being treated as investment instrument. The total number of brokers who are actively trading in regional stock exchanges have been less than the total membership. Most of the people who became members of these exchanges held these membership card as investment instruments just to sell them later on for considerable capital gains or appreciation and not for the purpose of operating their membership. Thus these membership were defunct and not functional. Least factor loading of .567 is observed in case of too few professionals. The respondents feel that presence of only few professionals as member brokers did not hamper the working system or contributed towards the betterment of the RSEs. Many of these professionals were not interested in contributing towards the working of the stock exchanges as they did not feel to be a part of the board which was much dominated by the politics of the regional stock exchanges and were averse to contribute towards the working systems of the RSEs.

4.4 SUGGESTIONS

The suggestions emerging out of the study includes the expert opinion and insights expressed on the relevant issues which are a part of this study. These specialists include stock exchange officials, brokers, capital market experts, academicians and so on. Thus these suggestions are the result of discussions carried out with these experts and their opinion as well as suggestions given on various issues are also a part of these suggestions. The suggestions are summarized as under:

1. All the RSEs may be given a regulatory mandate to consolidate and form a third stock Exchange, in addition to BSE and NSE.
2. All the previously listed companies should be given one time opportunity with a waiver of one time listing fees so that the same can get themselves listed once again on these exchanges and trading may assume in case of non-listed shares which are lying as idle capital with the investors of these regional exchanges, all over India.

   Such an endeavor would be an attempt to give opportunity to all the investors who may assume trading in non-listed or thinly traded shares.
3. As some of the RSEs may not be viable and/or interested in their revival, region-wise consolidation of RSEs should be facilitated.
4. The IndoNext, which is presently under the aegis of BSE, may be shifted and given to the "consolidated RSEs" under a unified trading platform and clearing corporation.
5. RSEs may be encouraged to consider any revival initiatives including corporate restructuring by merger with any of the premier stock exchanges subject to mutual agreement.
6. There is a felt need expressed for an active and liquid market for SMEs. The RSEs may not be able to survive independently in view of the changed

circumstances in the Indian securities market. Therefore, some of the RSEs which are interested, financially sound and compliant with the regulatory requirements may come together and set-up a common trading platform for such SMEs which have sound financials and viable business strategies.

7. In addition to providing specific trading platform for SMEs, the RSEs may be permitted to evolve an active market for marketing structured financial and investment products including mutual funds, insurance plans and other third party products apart from securitized instruments and derivative products.
8. That RSEs be permitted to diversify into other areas like conducting training programs for participants in capital market, providing services to investors, redressing investor complaints by acting as local forums of arbitration, distributing mutual fund products, acting as Registrar and Transfer Agents, providing securities lending and borrowing scheme and playing an advisory role to the SMEs in their need for capital creation. RSEs should be allowed to diversify into other areas of business like commodity exchange, Foreign exchange or other such suitable business through creation of a special purpose vehicle. They can also be the regional centres for SEBI.
9. RSEs may be permitted to establish a platform for book building, both for initial public offerings (IPOs) and also for delisting of companies.
10. The members of the RSEs who were also members of the national level stock exchanges, viz., BSE/NSE should not be allowed to be on the Board of the respective RSEs, as it results in a conflict of interest due to dual membership and hamper any developmental initiatives for the RSEs.
11. RSEs may be permitted to explore alternatives like Liaisoning with the other national level exchanges in their respective geographical locations, playing

the role as local/nodal centres for the national level exchanges and acting as an extended arm of such national level exchanges for functions like handling investor grievances/complaints, conducting training programmes in securities market, etc.

12. The subsidiaries of the regional stock exchanges should be considered to be on par with any other stock broker, thereby ensuring a level-playing field for all broking entities in all aspects like freedom of appointing franchisees, flexibility in appointment of directors on the board, enrolment of direct clients, executing proprietary trades.
13. The RSEs may be mandated to disassociate totally from the subsidiaries and the umbilical cord between the stock exchanges and their subsidiaries may be snapped. The subsidiaries shall be mandated to function as independent broking entities.
14. The subsidiaries should be permitted to operate in all areas of business apart from SMEs sector trading to forex trading, etc.
15. The scheme of Corporatisation and Demutualization mandates a divestment of at least 51% shareholding from trading members to the public or to the strategic investors.

    Presently, some of the RSEs are granted recognition on an annual basis. Such periodic recognition would create uncertainty in the minds of any prospective investor who is willing to take a stake in the RSE. Therefore, the RSEs should be granted permanent recognition so as to enable them to attract strategic investors during the process of divestment.
16. The Regulations to be notified by SEBI on divestment should provide for Foreign Direct investment (FDI) in RSEs, issuance of shares carrying differential voting rights, limited exercise of voting rights irrespective of the shareholding by an investor or strategic investor, etc.

17. SEBI should come out with clear guidelines providing permission to such RSEs which desire to exit the business of functioning as a stock exchange on a voluntary basis, spelling out the modalities for distribution of both financial and physical assets.
18. Post withdrawal of recognition, the surviving entity which becomes a regular company should be allowed to utilize the infrastructure for any other business purposes as deemed fit by that entity.
19. There could be companies which are exclusively listed only on a particular RSE which seeks voluntary withdrawal of recognition. Such companies should be allowed to get listing in the to be formed "consolidated RSE".
20. A multi-pronged approach is needed to improve liquidity in stocks. The share of retail investors in the public offer needs to be raised from 30 per cent to 40 per cent and the share of non-institutional investors be raised from 10 per cent to 15 per cent.
21. In respect of all thinly or marginally traded scrips, either specialists for each scrip, on the lines of the system in vogue in the New York Stock Exchange (all orders for sale and purchase of a scrip are matched by a single specialist) or at least two market-makers for each scrip need to be appointed by the issuer. Specialists/market-makers must be supplied with shares equivalent to at least one to two per cent of the public offer at the offer price in the case of shares to be listed and, in the case of shares already listed, at the average of the high and low of the weekly prices recorded in the preceding six months.

    Besides, specialists and market-makers need to be offered proper facilities for borrowing funds, preferably at a concessional rate applicable to borrowers in the priority sector. They may also be granted other financial assistance, such as waiver of transaction levy on market-making operations, and fiscal incentives in respect of profits and losses incurred in market-making transactions by way of treating profits/losses on short-term as long-term, as in the United States.

22. If the specialists and market-makers are unable to generate adequate liquidity in the traded securities then in such cases, a call auction system may be introduced, wherein all buy and sell orders that flow in a day or even a week can be matched at the closing of the period, with the bids and offers being continuously displayed. A similar system is in vogue in a few developed markets.
23. Companies whose shares are not traded even for a day and whose issued capital is less than Rs 3 crore should be directed to enhance their capital to at least Rs. 3 crore and the public shareholding to at least 25 per cent of the expanded equity capital, in addition to appointment of market-makers/specialists. A period of one year may be given to the companies. If they fail to comply with these requirements, shares of such companies should be de-listed after the shareholders concerned are given the option to exit, as per the SEBI guidelines relating to delisting of shares.
24. In a bid to enhance liquidity in illiquid stocks, the officials of regional exchanges have recommended appointment of market-makers and weekly settlement for thinly-traded stocks.
25. All companies coming up with IPOs should also be asked to appoint at least two market-makers continuously and on an ongoing basis till they come under A category, or become liquid.
26. The market-makers should get adequate incentives to make it attractive including no restriction on spreads between bids and offers by market-makers, access to information about the company, availability of low-cost finance and shares, besides other financial incentives like waiver of transaction levy and fiscal incentives for profits and losses from such deals.

27. Besides above recommendations certain additional measures for improving liquidity which include consolidated order books of various regional exchanges, call auction system where market-makers cannot be located, enhancement of minimum per centage of public offer to 40 per cent of the issued capital, suspension of book-building route for IPOs in favour of fixed price route and re-introduction of weekly settlement period in thinly-traded stocks *vis-à-vis* rolling settlement in thickly traded stocks may be introduced.

4.5 SCOPE FOR FUTURE RESEARCH

This study is an attempt to analyze the present conditions of the regional stock exchanges and to provide strategies for their revival.

The suggestions alongwith alternative business models suggested in the study leave enough scope for further research in the area of stock exchanges. Each alternative model of the stock exchange, discussed in this study can be taken upon as an independent area to understand the future of stock exchanges in India. The scope and concept of Indo Next Exchange which is a common platform for 15 regional stock exchanges in the country can also be a research area for any future study.

Appendix

QUESTIONNAIRE I
REGIONAL STOCK EXCHANGE (BROKERS)
(Ph.D. Research)

Dear Respondent,

I am pursuing my doctoral thesis on the topic "Strategies for Revival of Regional Stock Exchanges in India". I request you to kindly take some precious time from your busy schedule and thoughtfully fill up this questionnaire. The research and analysis of data shall only be used for purely academic purposes.

(Please use extra sheet where you feel space is inadequate for your observation/remarks).

Part I: Profile

Q. 1. Name of the Regional Stock Exchange.

____

Q. 2. How long are you associated with this exchange?

____

Q. 3. Are you individual or corporate broker?

____

Q. 4. How many branches do you have?

____

Q. 5. How many sub brokers do you have?

____

Q. 6. According to you whether RSE's are still relevant for Indian Capital Market?

____

____

____

Part II: Growth (Upward/Decline)

Q 7. (a): Has the RSE lived up to the expectation of investing population?

Yes ☐ No ☐

(b) If yes, please highlight the strengths of your Stock Exchange (kindly tick the appropriate strength according to you, you can tick more than one or all as per your opinion)

1. Easy reach to investors and brokers, etc. ( )
2. Physical Infrastructure ( )
3. Financial strength ( )
4. Meeting aspirations of small investors ( )
5. Managerial expertise ( )
6. Regional capital formation ( )

(c) If no, please highlight the weaknesses of your Stock Exchange (kindly tick the appropriate weakness according to you, you can tick more than one or all as per your opinion)

1. Limited number of companies for trading ( )
2. Non-Transparent and Inefficient trading and clearing mechanism. ( )
3. Poor quality of governance board ( )
4. Non-resolution of investor's grievance ( )
5. Inappropriate Technology ( )

Q. 8. To what factors will you attribute fall in business of your Exchange (please rank in order of importance with rank 1 to most important and so on)

1. Shift of investor's interest in large sized IPO's ( )
2. Diminishing growth due to government policy and SEBI's role ( )

3. Lack of good corporate governance by the exchange ( )
4. Poor quality Management of listed companies ( )
5. Growing problem of Illiquid/thinly traded stocks ( )
6. Lack of economic and industrial growth ( )
7. Loss of Investor faith in RSE's ( )
8. Preference of Investors to trade on large exchanges ( )
9. Less transparency in RSE's ( )
10. Any other (please specify)

____

Part III: Management Structure

Q. 9. If your Exchange is non-operative, what factors you feel have rendered it in- operative? Kindly rank in order of importance and elaborate. (Rank 1 to highest and so on)

1. Poor Governance ( )
2. Structural changes in financial markets ( )
3. Growing Problem of non-traded/thinly traded shares ( )
4. Decline in listing fee ( )
5. Competition ( )
6. Inappropriate Technology ( )
7. Loss of investor's faith in RSEs ( )

Any other (please indicate and rank ( )

____

____

____

Part IV: Revival

Q. 10. Do you plan to seek revival of your Exchange?

Yes ☐ No ☐

(a) If yes, which of the following activities or combination of activities would you recommend?

Reorganization Yes/No
Diversification Yes/No
New Businesses Yes/No
Any other____________________________

____

Would any of the above activities or combination of activities make the exchange economically viable? (please indicate) Yes/No

If yes to Re-organization, do you think the RSE's should have a tie-up with larger exchanges or merge to form an Independent larger exchange

____

____

____

____

____

Q. 11. If yes to Diversification and New Businesses, what areas of operation in your opinion should be pursued to enhance business at your Exchange? (kindly rank in order of importance with rank 1 being the most important and likewise)

1. Merchant/Investment Banking ( )
2. Commodities Trading ( )
3. Foreign Exchange Trading/SME Trading ( )
4. Marketing of Finance/Investment products ( )
5. Portfolio Management services ( )
6. Investor Education and courses
7. Operating as regional centers of NSE/BSE ( )
9. Providing dematerialization services ( )
10. Any other (please specify and rank. ( )

____

Q. 12. Do you look to Demutualization a Threat or Opportunity? (please elaborate)

____

____

____

____

Q. 13. Do you plan to come with an IPO?

Yes ☐ No ☐

If yes, what is the purpose for the same?

____

____

Q. 14. Do you think that the RSE's have a role in promoting equity cult and capital market?

Yes ☐ No ☐

Q. 15: Are you aware of the revival solutions adopted by RSE's in other Nations, having robust capital market?

Yes ☐ No ☐

(a) If yes what areas of concern you wish to address and how?

____

Q. 16. (a) Are you receptive to dilute your equity to foreign investor?

Yes ☐ No ☐

(b) If Yes, why____________________________

____

(c) If No, why____________________________

____

____

Q. 17. (a) Are you aware of the various initiatives taken by SEBI for revival of the RSE's?

Yes ☐ No ☐

Name of the respondent:..................................

Age: .... Marital status: single/married

Gender: Male/Female

Annual Income: < 2 lakh pa/< 5 lakh pa/> 5 lakh pa

Profession: salaried/business/professional/any other

Educational Qualifications: undergraduate/ graduate/post graduate/professionally qualified
Residence: rural/urban
Do you have access to internet: yes/no
Which newspaper and business magazines you prescribe:
....

I wish to place on record my heartfelt thanks for your having answered the above questionnaire in fulfilment of my doctoral thesis. Your observations and remarks shall help me in deducing a purposeful inference to my research.

Date: ....

QUESTIONNAIRE II

REGIONAL STOCK EXCHANGE (INVESTORS) (Ph.D. Research)

Dear Respondent,

I am pursuing my doctoral thesis on the topic "Strategies for Revival of Regional Stock Exchanges in India". I request you to kindly take some precious time from your busy schedule and thoughtfully fill up this questionnaire. The research and analysis of data shall only be used for purely academic purposes.

(Please use extra sheet where you feel space is inadequate for your observation/remarks) Opinion survey

Q. 1. Please mark the following attributes for the insufficient growth in market capitalization of RSE's

(a) low regional market size
Agree ☐ Strongly agree ☐
Disagree ☐ Strongly disagree ☐
Can't say ☐

(b) Too few listings
Agree ☐ Strongly agree ☐
Disagree ☐ Strongly disagree ☐
Can't say ☐

(c) Low quality of many listed companies
Agree ☐ Strongly agree ☐
Disagree ☐ Strongly disagree ☐
Can't say ☐

(d) Limited free float
Agree ☐ Strongly agree ☐
Disagree ☐ Strongly disagree ☐
Can't say ☐

Q. 2. Please mark the following attributes resulting in narrow base of investors at the RSE's

(a) Stagnation in number of shareholders
Agree ☐ Strongly agree ☐
Disagree ☐ Strongly disagree ☐
Can't say ☐

(b) Inadequate growth of unit holders in mutual funds

Agree ☐ Strongly agree ☐
Disagree ☐ Strongly disagree ☐
Can't say ☐

(c) Statutory minimal share ownership

Agree ☐ Strongly agree ☐
Disagree ☐ Strongly disagree ☐
Can't say ☐

(d) Lack of market education and awareness

Agree ☐ Strongly agree ☐
Disagree ☐ Strongly disagree ☐
Can't say ☐

(e) Lack of broad investor base to absorb IPO's

Agree ☐ Strongly agree ☐
Disagree ☐ Strongly disagree ☐
Can't say ☐

Q. 3. Please mark the following attributes with regards to lack of balance in governance structure at the RSE

(a) Weak professional management

Agree ☐ Strongly agree ☐
Disagree ☐ Strongly disagree ☐
Can't say ☐

(b) Ineffective regulation of members

Agree ☐ Strongly agree ☐
Disagree ☐ Strongly disagree ☐
Can't say ☐

(c) Ineffective regulation of listed companies

Agree ☐ Strongly agree ☐
Disagree ☐ Strongly disagree ☐
Can't say ☐

(d) Unequal access to corporate announcements

Agree ☐ Strongly agree ☐
Disagree ☐ Strongly disagree ☐
Can't say ☐

(e) Non-performance of outside Directors (Non-Member Directors)

Agree ☐ Strongly agree ☐
Disagree ☐ Strongly disagree ☐
Can't say ☐

Q. 4. Please mark the following attributes regarding fragmentation of capital market at the RSEs

(a) Division of Liquidity and Distortion of price discovery

Agree ☐ Strongly agree ☐
Disagree ☐ Strongly disagree ☐
Can't say ☐

(b) Cost inefficiency for all stakeholders

Agree ☐ Strongly agree ☐
Disagree ☐ Strongly disagree ☐
Can't say ☐

(c) Complexities in operations

Agree ☐ Strongly agree ☐
Disagree ☐ Strongly disagree ☐
Can't say ☐

(d) Lack of inter exchange competition

Agree ☐ Strongly agree ☐
Disagree ☐ Strongly disagree ☐
Can't say ☐

Q. 5. Please mark the following attributes towards insufficient economic capital at the RSE

(a) Limited revenue

Agree ☐ Strongly agree ☐
Disagree ☐ Strongly disagree ☐
Can't say ☐

(b) Inequitable burden sharing

Agree ☐ Strongly agree ☐
Disagree ☐ Strongly disagree ☐
Can't say ☐

(c) Low level of capital expenditure

Agree ☐ Strongly agree ☐
Disagree ☐ Strongly disagree ☐
Can't say ☐

(d) No financial guarantee

Agree ☐ Strongly agree ☐
Disagree ☐ Strongly disagree ☐
Can't say ☐

Q. 6. Please mark the following attributes for insufficient human capital resource development at the RSE

(a) Few professional

Agree ☐ Strongly agree ☐
Disagree ☐ . Strongly disagree ☐
Can't say ☐

(b) Lack of training and development

Agree ☐ Strongly agree ☐
Disagree ☐ Strongly disagree ☐
Can't say ☐

(c) Inability to develop new products and services

Agree ☐ Strongly agree ☐
Disagree ☐ Strongly disagree ☐
Can't say ☐

Q. 7. Please mark the following attributes for high degree speculation and concentration of business in few hands in RSEs

(a) Low levels of actual settlement

Agree ☐ Strongly agree ☐
Disagree ☐ Strongly disagree ☐
Can't say ☐

(b) Concentration of liquidity and market capitalization

Agree ☐ Strongly agree ☐
Disagree ☐ Strongly disagree ☐
Can't say ☐

(c) Dominance of Badla financing

Agree ☐ Strongly agree ☐
Disagree ☐ Strongly disagree ☐
Can't say ☐

(d) Excessive volatility

Agree ☐ Strongly agree ☐
Disagree ☐ Strongly disagree ☐
Can't say ☐

Q. 8. Please mark the following attributes with regard to large number and low quality of intermediaries

(a) Weak criteria to become a member

Agree ☐ Strongly agree ☐
Disagree ☐ Strongly disagree ☐
Can't say ☐

(b) Weak criteria to become a broker

Agree ☐ Strongly agree ☐
Disagree ☐ Strongly disagree ☐
Can't say ☐

(c) Weak criteria to become a market maker

Agree ☐ Strongly agree ☐
Disagree ☐ Strongly disagree ☐
Can't say ☐

(d) Barrier to entry of new intermediaries

Agree ☐ Strongly agree ☐
Disagree ☐ Strongly disagree ☐
Can't say ☐

(e) Membership card treated as investment instrument

Agree ☐ Strongly agree ☐
Disagree ☐ Strongly disagree ☐
Can't say ☐

(f) Low capitalization of brokers

Agree ☐ Strongly agree ☐
Disagree ☐ Strongly disagree ☐
Can't say ☐

(g) A single class of brokers

Agree ☐ Strongly agree ☐
Disagree ☐ Strongly disagree ☐
Can't say ☐

Q. 9: Please mark for "Inadequate investor protection" attribute at the RSE's

Agree ☐ Strongly agree ☐
Disagree ☐ Strongly disagree ☐
Can't say ☐

Name of the respondent: ....
Age: .... Marital status: single/married..........................
Gender: Male/Female..
Annual Income: < 2 lakh pa/< 5 lakh pa/> 5 lakh pa
Profession: salaried/business/professional/any other
Educational Qualifications: undergraduate/graduate/post-graduate/professionally qualified
Residence: rural/urban....................................... Do you have access to internet: yes/no ....
Which newspaper and business magazines you prescribed
....

I wish to place on record my heartfelt thanks for your having answered the above questionnaire in fulfilment of my doctoral thesis. Your observations and remarks shall help me in deducing a purposeful inference to my research.

Date: ....

BIBLIOGRAPHY

Agarwal, P.C. (1992), "Suggestions on Scripless Trading", *Chartered Secretary*, Vol. 22, No. 10 (Oct.), p. 888.

Agrawal, G.D. (1992), "Mutual Funds and Investors' Interest", *Chartered Secretary*, Vol. 22, No. 1 (Jan.), p. 23.

Alverez, Ana Maria, and Kalotay Kalman., 2008, "Emerging Stock Markets and the Scope for Regional Cooperation," United Nations Conference on Trade and Development Discussion Paper No. 79 (Geneva: UNCTAD).

Amihud, Yakov and Haim Mendelson, "Asset Pricing and the Bid-Ask Spread," *Journal of Financial Economics*, Vol. II, 2005.

Anshuman, A.S. and Prakash Chandra, R. (1996), "Small Equity Shareholdings : The Repurcussions", *Chartered Secretary*, Vol. 21, No. 7, p. 562.

Atje, Raymond and Boyan Jovanic, 1993, "Stock markets and Development," *European Economic Review*, Vol. 37 (April), pp. 632-40.

Atmaramani, K.A. (1984), "Issue of Non-Convertible Debentures by Public Limited Companies", *Chartered Secretary*, Vol. 14, No. 7 (Jul.), pp. 463-68.

Avadhani V A(1992), Investment and Securities Markets in India: *Investment Management*, Himalaya Publishing, Bombay, p. 426.

Ayuso, J. and R. Blanco (2000), Has financial market integration increased during the nineties? Ban code Espana service de estudios, document de trabajon 9923.

Bal, R.K., Mishra, B.B. (1990), "Role of Mutual Funds in Developing Indian Capital Market", *Indian Journal of Commerce*, Vol. XLIII, p. 1 [illegible].

Balasubramaniam, C.S. (1980), "Indexes of Ordinary Share Prices—An Evaluation", *Artha Vijnana*, Vol. 22 No. 4 (Dec.), pp. 552-64.

Balasubramaniam, N. (1993), Corporate Financial Policies and Shareholders Returns: The Indian Experience, Himalaya Publishing, Bombay, p. 266.

Balkrishnan (1984), "Determinants of Equity Prices in India", *Management Accountant*, Vol. 19, No. 12 (Dec.), pp. 728-30.

Barua, S.K. (1980), "Valuation of Securities and Influence of Value on Financial Decision of a Firm", Doctoral Dissertation, Indian Institute of Management, Ahmedabad.

Barua, S.K. (1981), "Short-run Price Behaviour of Securities: Some Evidence of Indian Capital", *Vikalpa* (Apr..-Jun.) Vol. 6, No. 2, p. 93-100.

Barua, S.K. (1987), "Some Observations on the Report of the High Powered Committee on Stock Exchange Reforms", Annual Issue of ICFAI, December 1987.

Barua, S.K. (1993), "SEBI's Regulatory, priorities: Need for Change", Unpublished, Paper for the Ministry of Finance, Indian Institute of Management, Ahmedabad.

Barua, S.K. and Raghunathan, V. (1982), "Inflation Hedge in India—Stocks or Bullion", Working Paper No. 429, (July-Sept.), Indian Institute of Management, Ahmedabad.

Barua, S.K. and Raghunathan, V. (1986), "Inefficiency of the Indian Capital Market", *Vikalpa*, Vol. 11, No. 3 (Jul.-Sept.), pp. 225-30.

Barua, S.K. and Raghunathan, V. (1987), "Inefficiency and Speculation in the Indian Capital Market", *Vikalpa*, Vol. 12, No. 3 (Jul.-Sept.), pp. 53-58.

Barua, S.K. and Raghunathan, V. (1988), "Testing Stock Market Efficiency Using Risk-Return Parity Rule : A Reply (Notes and Comments)", *Vikalpa*, Vol. 13, (Jul.-Sept.), pp. 82-83.

Barua, S.K. and Raghunathan, V. (1990), "Convertible Securities and Implied Options", *Vikalpa*, Vol. 15, No. 4 (Oct.-Dec.), pp. 23-28.

Barua, S.K. and Raghunathan, V. (1990), "Soaring Stock Prices: Defying Fundamentals", *Economic and Political Weekly*, Vol. 25, No. 46, Nov. 17, pp. 2559-61.

Barua, S.K. and Srinivasan, G. (1982), "Experiment on Individual Investment Decision-making Process", Working Paper No. 423, (Apr..-June), Indian Institute of Management, Ahmedabad.

Barua, S.K. and Srinivasan, G. (1987), "Investigation of Decision Criteria for Investment in Risky Assets", *OMEGA: International Journal of Management Science*, Vol. 15, No. 3, pp. 247-53.

Barua, S.K. and Srinivasan, G. (1987), "Setting the Terms for Convertible Debenture Issues : Should the Spirit of Company Law be Violated?", *Vikalpa*, Vol. 12, No. 1, (Jan.-Mar.), pp. 57-61.

Barua, S.K. and Srinivasan, G. (1988), "The Decision Process of Individuals under Conditions of Risk : An Experimental Study, *International Journal of Management*, Vol. 5, No. 3, (Sept.), pp. 251-58.

Barua, S.K. and Srinivasan, G. (1991), "Experiment on Individual Investment Decision-making Process", *Sankhya*, Vol. 53, Series B, pp. 74-88.

Barua, S.K. and Varma, J.R. (1990), "Mastershares : Enigmatic Performance", Working Paper No. 906, (Oct.-Dec.), Indian Institute of Management, Ahmedabad.

Barua, S.K. and Varma, J.R. (1991), "Indian Convertible Bonds with Unspecified Terms: A Valuation Model", Working Paper No. 991, (Jul.-Sept.), Indian Institute of Management, Ahmedabad.

Barua, S.K. and Varma, J.R. (1991), "Mastershares: A Bonanza for Large Investors", *Vikalpa*, Vol. 16, No. 1 (Jan..-Mar.), pp. 29-34.

Barua, S.K. and Varma, J.R. (1991), "Mastershares: Market Prices Divorced from Fundamentals", Working Paper No. 953, (Jul.-Sep.), Indian Institute of Management, Ahmedabad.

Barua, S.K. and Varma, J.R. (1992), "Gorbachev Betas : The Russian Coup and The Market Blues", Working Paper No. 1054, (Jul.-Sept.), Indian Institute of Management, Ahmedabad.

Barua, S.K. and Varma, J.R. (1993), "RBI Autonomy and the Indian Financial Sector", *Vikalpa,* Vol. 18, No. 4 (Oct.-Dec.), pp. 15-19.

Barua, S.K. and Varma, J.R. (1993), "Securities Scam: Genesis, Mechanics and Impact", *Vikalpa,* Vol. 18, No. 1 (Jan.-Mar.), pp. 3-12.

Barua, S.K. and Varma, J.R. (1993), "Speculative Dynamics: The Case of Mastershares", *Advances in Financial Planning and Forecasting,* Vol. 5, Jai Press, Greenwitch, CT, USA.

Barua, S.K. and Varma, J.R. (1993), The Great Indian Scam: Story of the Missing Rs. 4000 crore, Vision Books, Delhi, p. 160.

Barua, S.K. and Varma, J.R. (1993), The Great Indian Scam: Story of the Missing Rs. 4000 crore, Vision Books, Delhi, p. 160.

Barua, S.K., Madhavan, T. and Raghunathan, V. (1987), "Implications of Changes in the Holding, period and other parameters on Systematic Risk and Performance of a Security", Working Paper No. 664, (Jan.-Mar.), Indian Institute of Management, Ahmedabad.

Barua, S.K., Madhavan, T. and Varma, J.R. (1991), "Indian Convertible Bonds with Unspecified Terms: An Empirical Study", Working Paper No. 990, (Oct.-Dec.), Indian Institute of Management, Ahmedabad.

Barua, S.K., Raghunathan, V. and Varma, J.R. (1992), Portfolio Management, Tata McGraw-Hill, New Delhi, p. 256.

Barua, S.K., Raghunathan, V., Venkiteswaran, N. and Varma, J.R. (1994), "Analysis of the Indian Securities Industry: Market for Debt", Working Paper No. 1164, Indian Institute of Management, Ahmedabad.

Barua, S.K., Varma, J.R. and Venkiteswaran, N. (1991), "A Regulatory Framework for Mutual Funds", *Economic and Political Weekly,* Review of Management and Industry, Vol. 26, No. 21, May 25, pp. 55-59.

Basu, Debasish and Dalal, Sucheta (1993), Scam: Who Won, Who Lost, Who Got Away, UBS Publishers and Distributors, New Delhi, p. 294.

Benimadhu, Sunil, CEO, Stock Exchange of Mauritius Review, January, 2002.

Bhalla, U.K. (1983), Investment Managem : Security Analysis and Portfolio Management, S. and, New Delhi, p. 391.

Bhat, Ramesh (1988), "Market-wide Commonalities in Corporate Earnings and Significance Tests of Accounting Betas", Working Paper No. 750 (Apr.-Jun.), Indian Institute of Management, Ahmedabad.

Bhat, Ramesh and Pandey, I.M. (1997), "Efficient Market Hypothesis : Understanding and Acceptance in India", Working Paper No. 691, (Jul.-Sept.), Indian Institute of Management, Ahmedabad.

Bhat. Ramesh (1988), "An Empirical Study of the Intertemporal Relations Among the Regional Share Price Indicators", Working Paper No. 748, (Apr.-Jun.), Indian Institute of Management, Ahmedabad.

Bhatt, M.C. (1980), "Merchant Banking in India : Its Contribution to National Development", *Chartered Secretary*, Vol. 10, No. 10, (Oct.), p. 922.

Bhatt, Ramesh K. (1981), "Pitfalls of the Price-Earnings Ratio", *Chartered Accountant*, Vol. 30, (July), p. 19.

Bhattacharya, C.D. (1981), "Variance Analysis to chances in return of Investment", Working Paper No. 365 (Apr.-Jun.), Indian Institute of Management, Ahmedabad.

Bhole, L.M. (1974), Investment, Interest and Monetary Policy in India, Bombay University, Bombay.

Bhole, L.M. (1980), "Retained Earnings, Dividends and Share Prices of Indian Joint Stock Companies", *Economic and Political Weekly*, Review of Management, (Aug.), pp. M92-100.

Bhole, L.M. (1982), Financial Markets and Institutions : Growth Structure and Innovations, Tata McGraw Hill, New Delhi, p. 360, Ist edition.

Bhole, L.M. (1982), Financial Markets and Institutions : Growth Structure and Innovations, Tata McGraw Hill, New Delhi, p. 360, Ist edition.

Bhole, L.M. (1992), "Proposals for Financial Sector Reforms in India: An Appraisal (Perspectives)", *Vikalpa*, Vol. 17, No. 3 (Jul.-Sept.), pp. 3-9.

Bhole, L.M. (1992), "Proposals for Financial Sector Reforms in India : An Appraisal (Perspectives)", *Vikalpa*, Vol. 17, No. 3 (Jul.-Sep.), p. 3-9.

Bhole, L.M. (1992), Financial Institutions and Markets : Structure Growth and Innovations, IInd Edition, Tata McGraw Hill, Delhi, p. 527.

Chandra, Prasanna (1977), "Comparison of the Additive and Multiplicative Models of Stock Valuation", *Decision*, Vol. 4, No. 1 (Jan.).

Chandra, Prasanna (1989), "Individual Portfolio Management: Mistakes and Remedies", *Chartered Financial Analyst*, (Sep.-Oct.), pp. 3-5.

Chandra, Prasanna (1989), "Pricing of Public Issues", *Chartered Financial Analyst*, (Jul.-Aug.), pp. 3-7.

Chandra, Prasanna (1990), "Indian Capital Market : Pathways of Development", *ASCI Journal of Management*, Vol. 20, No. 2-3 (Sept.-Dec.), pp. 129-37.

Chandra, Prasanna (1990), Investment Game: How to Win, Tata McGraw-Hill, New Delhi (1990), p. 230.

Chaudhury, S.K. (1985), "Convertible Debenture : Analysing Yield and Risk", *Management Accountant*, Vol. 20, No. 1 (Jan.), pp. 86-88.

Chaudhury, S.K. (1991), "Sesonality in Share Returns: Preliminary Evidence on Day-of-the-Week Effect", *Chartered Accountant*, Vol. 40, No. 5 (Nov), p. 407.

Chaudhury, S.K. (1991), "Short Run Behaviour of Industrial Share Price Indices : An Empirical Study of Returns, Volatility and Covariance Structure", *Prajanan*, Vol. XX, Apr.-Jun., No. 2, pp. 99-113.

Chaudhury, S.K. (1991), "Short-run Share Price Behaviour : New Evidence on Weak form of Market Efficiency", *Vikalpa*, Vol. 16, No. 4 (Oct.-Dec.), pp. 17-21.

Chawla, O.P. (1989), Money And Securities Markets: Emerging Trends, NIBM Pune Conference Papers (Ed).

Datar, P.A. (1985), "Valuation of Bonus Shares", *Chartered Secretary*, Vol. XV, No. 3 (March), p. 156.

Dhankar, J.N. (1986), A Treatise on Merchant Banking, Project Approval and Financing, Skylark Publications, New Delhi.

Dhillon, N. (1993), "Market Regulations and Stock Market Activity", Doctoral Dissertation, Indian Institute of Management, Ahmedabad.

Dholakia, R.H. and Bhatt, Ramesh (1986), "Dividend Rate and Variation in Share Prices: An Exploration into their Inter-relationship", Working Paper No. 638, Indian Institute of Management, Ahmedabad.

Dilbagh, S.B. (1991), "Indian Stock Market Seasonality : A Note", *Indian Economic Journal,* Vol 39, No. 2, (Oct.-Dec.), pp. 110-19.

Dixit, R.K. (1984), "The Behaviour of Share Price in India", Doctoral Dissertation, Panjab University, Chandigarh.

Dixit, R.K. (1986), Behaviour of Share Prices and Investment in India, Deep and Deep Publications, New Delhi, p. 328.

Francis, C.K. (1991), "SEBI—The Need of the Hour", SEDME, Vol. 18(3), pp. 37-41.

Francis, C.K. (1991), "Towards a Healthy Capital Market", *Yojana,* Vol. 35, Mar. 1-15, pp. 11-13.

Gahan, P. (1985), "Short term Investment vs Disinvestment under conditions of Certainity—A Decision-making Approach", *The Indian Journal of Commerce,* Vol. 39, No. 4.

Ganesh, R. (1988), "Return on Net Worth : A Close Look", *Chartered Secretary,* Vol. 18 (9), pp. 774-78.

Gujarathi, M. and Srinivasan, G. (1980), "Shareholders Discount Coupons—A Case of Disguised Dividends", *Chartered Accountant,* Vol. 27, No. 9, March, pp. 833-36.

Gujarathi, Mahendra (1987), "Do New Equity Issues fetch Extranormal Returns?", *Vikalpa,* Vol. 12, No. 4 (Oct.-Dec.), pp. 43-50.

Gupta, L.C. (1978), "Bonus Shares: Facts, Fiction and Policy", *Chartered Accountant,* Vol. 27, No 2, pp. 85-90.

Gupta, L.C. (1980), "Long-term Rates of Return on Industrial Equities in India", *Economic and Political Weekly,* Review of Management, August, pp. M85-M92.

Gupta, L.C. (1981), Rates of Return on Equities: The Indian Experience, Oxford University Press, New Delhi.

Gupta, L.C. (1987), Shareholders' Survey : Geographic Distrubution, Manas Publications, Delhi., p. 86.

Gupta, L.C. (1991), Indian Shareholders : A Survey, Society for Capital Market Research and Development, Delhi, p. 174.

Gupta, L.C. (1992), Stock Exchange Trading in India : Agenda for Reform, Society for Capital Market Research and Development, Delhi, p. 123.

Gupta, L.C. (1992), Stock Exchange Trading in India : Agenda for Reform, Society for Capital Market Research and Development, Delhi, p. 123.

Gupta, O.P. (1980), "A Case for Convertible Debenture", *Chartered Secretary*, Vol 10, No. 5, (May), pp. 464-66.

Gupta, O.P. (1985), Behaviour of Share Prices in India: A Test of Market Efficiency, National, New Delhi.

Gupta, O.P. (1989), Stock Market Efficiency and Price Behaviour (The Indian Experience), Anmol Publications, New Delhi, p. 373.

Gupta, Ramesh (1987), "Is the Indian Capital Market Inefficient of Excessively Speculative?", *Vikalpa*, Vol. 12, No. 2 (Apr.-Jun.), pp. 21-28.

Gupta, Ramesh (1991), "Portfolio Management : The Process and Its Dynamics", Working Paper No. 923, (Jan.-Mar.), The Indian Institute of Management, Ahmedabad.

Gupta, Ramesh (1991), "Regulation of Securities Market in India: Some Issues ", *Chartered Secretary*, Vol. 21, No. 6 (Jun.).

Gupta, Ramesh (1991), "Revamping Stock Exchange Operations—Some Suggestions", Working Paper No. 922, (Jan.-Mar.), Indian Institute of Management, Ahmedabad.

Gupta, Ramesh (1991), "Revamping Stock Exchange Operations—Some Suggestions", Working Paper No. 922, (Jan.-Mar.), Indian Institute of Management, Ahmedabad.

Gupta, Ramesh (1992), "Development of the Capital Market in India: A Regulatory Perspective", Working Paper No. 997, (Jan.-Mar.), Indian Institute of Management, Ahmedabad.

Gupta, Ramesh (1992), "Foreign Stock Listing: Benefits and Costs", *Chartered Secretary,* Vol. 22, No. 5 (May), pp. 410-11.

Gupta, Ramesh (1992), "Options Trading: A Primer and a Proposal", *Chartered Secretary,* Vol. 22, No. 10 (Oct.), p. 883.

Gupta, Renu (2002), "Performance Evaluation of National Stock Exchange of India ", A Ph.D. thesis submitted to Department of Commerce and Business Studies, Jamia Milia Islamia University, New Delhi.

Gupta, S.M. (1991), "Behavioural Practices of Bonus Issues", *Chartered Accountant,* Vol 39, No. 12, p. 1010.

Gurley, J. and E. Shaw, 1955, "Financial aspects of Economic Development," *Americam Economic Review,* Vol. 45, pp. 515-38.

Ignatius, Roger (1992), "The Bombay Stock Exchange : Seasonalities and Investment Oppurtunities", *Indian Economic Review,* Vol. XXVII, No. 2, pp. 223-27.

Jain, P.K. (1979), "UTI and The New Issue Market", *Artha Vijnana,* Vol. 21, No. 2 (June), p. 218.

James, Riedel (1999): "Capital Market Integration in Developing Asia", Blackwell Publishers Ltd.

Jhamb, Mahendra (1991), "Mutual Funds Dominate Market Capital", *Yojana,* Vol. 35, July 15, pp. 8-9.

Kapadia, M.B. (1981), "Financing with Convertible Debentures", *Management Accountant,* Vol. 16, No. 11, (Nov.), p. 534.

Kapoor, R.C. (1981), "Convertible Debentures : Major Financial Considerations", *Management Accountant,* Vol. 16, No. 7, (Jul.), p. 321.

Kothari, Rajesh (1986), "Profile of Recent Developments in Indian Capital Market", *Prashanika,* HCM-RIPA, Vol. XV, No. 4 (Oct.-Dec.).

Lal, Jawahar (1992), "Investors' Understanding of Information: Some Evidence", *Chartered Secretary,* Vol. 22, No. 3 (Mar.), p. 211.

Lal, T. (1990), "Primary Capital Market : Some Reflections", *Yojana,* Vol. 34, June 16-30, pp. 9-12.

Mahapatra, R.P. and Sahu, P.K. (1993), "A Note on Determinants of Corporate Dividend Behaviour in India—An Econometric Analysis", *Decision*, Vol. 20(1), pp. 1-22.

Nath, G.C. and Verma, S. (2006), Study of Common Stochastic Trend and Co-integration in the Emerging Markets: A Case Study of India, Singapore and Taiwan", Research Paper, NSE-India.

Obaidullah, M. (1992), "How do Stock Prices React to Bonus Issues?", *Vikalpa*, Vol. 17, No. 1 (Jan.-Mar.), pp. 17-22.

Okeahalam, Charles C. (2006), "Strategic Alliances and Mergers of Financial Exchanges: The Case of the SADC," Paper presented at the fourth annual conference of the Centre for the Study of African Economies, Oxford University, March 29-31, 2006.

Palaha, Satinder (1991), Cost of Capital and Corporate, Policy, with Special Reference to the Influence of Changes in Accounting Variables on Stock Prices, Anmol Publications, New Delhi, p. 186.

Pandey, I.M. (1981), Capital Structure and the Cost of Capital, Vikas, New Delhi.

Pandya, V.H. (1992), "Securities and Exchange Board of India: Its Role, Powers, Functions and Activities", *Chartered Secretary*, Vol. 22, No. 9 (Sept.), p. 783.

Pasricha, S.N. (1979), "Fixed Investment Behaviour in India—A Survey of Econometric Studies", *Margin*, Vol 12, pp. 115-30.

Prabhakaran, Malathy (1989), "Do Equities Act as a Hedge against Inflation?", *Economic and Political Weekly*, Vol. 24, No. 8, Feb. 25, pp. 24-26.

Puranik, Alok (1992), "Role of Corporate Securities in Household Saving and Private Corporate Sector Financing during Eighties—Some Empirical Observations", *Chartered Secretary*, Vol. 22, No. 11 (Nov), p. 991.

Raghunathan, V. (1991), Stock Exchanges and Investments: Straight Answers to 100 Nagging Questions, Tata McGraw Hill, New Delhi, p. 176.

Raghunathan, V. and Srinivasan, G. (1985), "Investment Opportunities and Gordon's Stock Valuation Model—A Note", Working Paper No. 588, (Oct.-Dec.), Indian Institute of Management, Ahmedabad.

Raghunathan, V. and Srinivasan, G. (1987), "Target Debt Maintanence Under Alternative Net Present Value Specifications and Implications for Investment and Finance Decisions", Working Paper No. 669, (Apr.-Jun.), Indian Institute of Management, Ahmedabad.

Raghunathan, V. and Varma, J.R. (1991), "Market Valuation Model Under Differential Taxes, Inflation, Recurring Investments and Flotation Costs", Working Paper No. 956, (Jul.-Sep.), Indian Institute of Management, Ahmedabad.

Raghunathan, V., Varma, J.R. (1992), "Crisil Rating : When Does AAA mean B?", *Vikalpa*, Vol. 17, No. 2 (Apr.-Jun.), pp. 35-42.

Raghunathan, V., Varma, J.R. (1992), "Why the Dollars do not Flow into India", Unpublished Paper, Indian Institute of Management, Ahmedabad.

Raghunathan, V., Varma, J.R. (1993), "When AAA Means B: The State of Credit Rating in India", Working Paper No. 1141, Indian Institute of Management, Ahmedabad.

Raghunathan, V., Varma, J.R. and Venkiteswaran, N. (1991), "The New Economic Package and the Agenda for the Restructuring the Financial Sector (Perspectives)", *Vikalpa*, Vol. 16, No. 3 (Jul.-Sep.), pp. 3-11.

Ramachandran, G. (1989), "Behaviour of Share Prices—A Statistical Analysis", Doctoral Dissertation, Institute for Financial Management and Research.

Ramachandran, G. (1992), "Information Content of Bonus Issues—An Empirical Analysis in the Indian Context", Working Paper Series, January, Unit Trust of India.

Ramachandran, K.S. (1993), Scanning the Scam: How and Why of the Securities Scandal, NEO Publishing Company, New Delhi, p. 199.

Ranganatham, M. and Subramanian, V. (1993), "Weak Form of Efficient Markets Hypothesis : A Spectral Analytical Investigation", *Vikalpa*, Vol. 18, No. 2 (Apr.-Jun.)

Rao, Narayana K.V.S.S. and Bhole, L.M. (1990), "Inflation and Equity Returns", *Economic and Political Weekly*, Vol. 25, No. 21, May 26, pp. M-91-M-96.

Saha, A. (2002), "Merchant Banking : Retrospect and Prospects", *Yojana*, Vol XVII, No 1, 1988, pp. 61-79.

Sahni, S.K. (1985), Stock Exchanges in India: Practices, Problems, Prospects, North Publishing Corporation, New Delhi, p. 344.

Sankar, T.L., Mishra, R.K. and Nandagopal, R. (1992), "Credit Rating: A New Concept in Security Analysis in India", *Chartered Secretary*, Vol. 22, No. 5 (May), pp. 412-15.

Sankaran, Venkateshwar (1991), "The Relationship of Indian Stock Market to Other Stock Markets", *Indian Economic Journal*, Vol. 39, No. 2 (Oct.-Dec.), pp. 105-09.

Sarma, S. Narasimha (1993), Financial Economics of Bonus Shares: Implications for the Value of the Firm, Academic Foundation, Delhi, p. 144.

Shah, Ajay (2005), Interest Rate Volatility and Risk in Indian Banking (January 2005), IMF Working Paper, pp. 1-28, 2005.

Sharma, J.L. (1983), "Efficient Capital Markets and Random Character of Stock Prices Behaviour in a Developing Economy", *Indian Journal of Economics*, Vol. 63, No. 251 (Oct.-Dec.), p. 395.

Simha, S.L.N., Hemalatha, D. and Balakrishnan, S. (1979), Investment Management, Institute of Financial Management and Research, Madras.

Singh, Preeti (1986), Investment Management : Security Analysis and Portfolio Management, Himalaya Publishing, Bombay, p. 579.

Singh, Sukhdev (1990), "Convertible Debentures—An Increasing Trend", *Chartered Secretary*, Vol. XX, No. 8 (Aug.), p. 644.

Sinha, N. (1983), "Convertible Debentures—An Analytical Study", *Chartered Accountant*, Vol. 31, No. 3 (Sept.), p. 222.

Sinha, Sidharth (1992), "The High Price-Earnings Ratio in the Indian Stock Market and Investment by Foreign

Financial Institutions", Unpublished Paper, Indian Institute of Management, Ahmedabad.

Sinha, Sidharth (1993), "The Badla Market and Futures and Options", Unpublished Paper, Indian Institute of Management, Ahmedabad (pending presentation in CBOT, Fifth Annual Asia-Pacific Futures Research Symposium, March 14/15, 1994, Taipei).

Srinivas, Akella R. and Greenbaum, Stuart I.. (1992), "Innovations in Interest Rates, Duration Transformation and Bank Stock Returns", *Journal of Money, Credit and Banking*, Vol. 24(1), pp. 24-42.

Srinivasan, N.P. and Narasimhan, M.S. (1988), "Testing Stock Market Efficiency using Risk-return Parity Rule (Notes and Comments)", *Vikalpa*, Vol. 13, (Apr.-Jun.), pp. 61-66.

Srinivasan, R. (1993) "Security Prices Behaviour Associated with Rights: Issue-Related Events", Doctoral Dissertation, Indian Institute of Management, Ahmedabad.

Srinivasan, S. (1988), "Testing of Capital Assets, Pricing Model in Indian Environment", *Decision*, Vol 15, (Jan.-Mar.), p. 51.

Srivastava, R.M. (1984), "Testing Modigliani—Millers Dividend Valuation Model in Indian Context—A Case Study of 327 Joint Stock Companies", *Management Accountant*, Vol. 19, No. 11, (Nov.), pp. 641-42.

Srivastava, R.M. (1991), "Merchant Banking In India - A Bright Future", *Yojana*, Vol. 35, May 15, pp. 12-13.

Subramaniam, S. (1989), "The Impact of Political and Economic Events on Stock Behaviour", Doctoral Dissertation, Indian Institute of Management, Ahmedabad.

Sundaram, S.M. (1991), "Soaring Stock Prices", *Economic and Political Weekly*, Vol. 26, No. 18, May 4, p. 1184.

Trikha, Kapil (2004), "Merchant Bankers and Public Issues", *Chartered Accountant*, Vol. 38, No. 6 (Dec.), p. 477.

Tripathy, Nalini Prava (2008): "Towards Integration of Developed Markets and World Market: Empirical Evidence", *The ICFAI Journal of Applied Finance*, Vol. 12, No. 8, 2008.

Varma, J.R. (1988), "Asset Pricing Models Under Parameter Non-Stationarity", Doctoral Dissertation, Indian Institute of Management, Ahmedabad.

Varma, J.R. (1989), "Equilibrium Pricing of Special Bearer Bonds", Working Paper No. 817, (Jul.-Sept.), Indian Institute of Management, Ahmedabad.

Varma, J.R. (1992), "Is the BSE Sensitive Index Better than the National Index?", Working Paper No. 988, (Oct.-Dec.), Indian Institute of Management, Ahmedabad.

Varma, J.R. and Barua, S.K. (1988), "Estimation Errors and Time Varying Betas in Event Studies—A New Approach", Working Paper No. 759, (Jul.-Sept.), Indian Institute of Management, Ahmedabad.

Varma, J.R. and Venkiteswaranm N. (1990), "Guidelines on Share Valuation : How Fair is Fair Value?", *Vikalpa*, Vol. 15, No. 4 (Oct.-Dec.), pp. 3-10.

Varma, J.R., Raghunathan, Korwar, A. and Bhatt, M.C. (1992), "The Narasimham Committee Report—Some Future Ramifications and Suggestions", Working Paper No. 1009, (Jan.-Mar.), Indian Institute of Management, Ahmedabad.

Varma, J.R., Raghunathan, V. and Bhatt, M.C. (1992), "Comments on SEBI's Draft Takeover Code", Working Paper No. 1010, (Jan.-Mar.), Indian Institute of Management, Ahmedabad.

Verma, J.C. (1990), Merchant Banking : Organisation and Management, Tata McGraw Hill, New Delhi, p. 354.

Vidhyashankar, S. (1990), "Mutual Funds—Emerging Trends in India", *Chartered Secretary*, Vol. XX, No. 8 (Aug.), p. 639.

Yalawar, Y.B. (1988), "Bombay Stock Exchange : Rates of Return and Efficiency", *Indian Economic Journal*, Vol. 35, No. 4 (Apr.-Jun.), pp. 68-121.

Yasaswy, N.J. (1992), PSU Stocks Picking the Winners, Vision Books, New Delhi, p. 206.

Yoon, S. Park (2002): "Characters and Measurement Indicators of International Financial Integration in Developing Countries". George Washington University, Washington D.C., Feb. 1999.

Zahir, M.A. and Khanna, Yakesh (1982), "Determinants of Stock Prices in India", *Chartered Accountant*, Vol. 30, No. 8 (Feb.).

Websites

http://www.world-exchanges.org/
http://www.sebi.gov.in
http://www.bseindia.com
http://www.nseindia.com

Index